MW00681484

**Required Reading Range
Course Reader**

Fairchild Books

An imprint of Bloomsbury Publishing Plc

50 Bedford Square	175 Fifth Avenue
London	New York
WC1B 3DP	NY 10010
UK	USA

www.bloomsbury.com

First published 2013

British Library Cataloging-in-Publication Data
A catalogue record for this book is available from the British Library.

ISBN: PB: 978-2-940496-04-4
ePDF: 978-2-940447-56-5

Bloomsbury Cataloging-in-Publication Data
Sherin, Aaris
Sustainable Thinking: Ethical approaches to design and design management/
Aaris Sherin p.cm
Includes bibliographic references and index.
ISBN 978-2-940496-04-4 (pbk.) – ISBN 978-2-940447-56-5 (ePDF)
1. Sustainable design – Study and teaching.
2. Sustainability – Study and teaching.
3. Design – Social aspects.
NK1520 .S547 2013

Designed by DGA Vienna
Printed and bound in China

Cover image courtesy of Chris Haughton

Sustainable Thinking

Ethical approaches to design and design management

**Required Reading Range
Course Reader**

Aaris Sherin

Introduction

Sustainability and ethics are reshaping the way design is practised and applied in non-profit organizations and corporate settings. Designers who can serve the needs of specific populations, work in different contexts, and reimagine the use and reuse of resources are increasingly in demand by clients who are looking for outputs that minimize their impact on the planet, while maintaining their competitive advantage. These designers combine innovative creative thinking with analytical problem-solving skills to produce outputs that are business ready and ethically driven.

In addition to the ability to visualize new and innovative solutions to stated problems, there is a need for design professionals who can identify appropriate outcomes in more complex and less defined situations. In such instances, a design consultant or team may be brought in to identify previously unknown needs or create strategies that will use design outputs to alter an audience's perception of a product, action or event. Values-driven design requires leaders who are able to use traditional design competencies in visionary ways, and who can work with a diverse set of stakeholders to solve universal design problems.

Designing with values in mind

Sustainability has emerged as a defining characteristic of the first decade of the twenty-first century. It connects like-minded people, crosses cultural and geographic boundaries, and has prompted businesses and governments to rethink their mission and policies. Unlike the environmental movement of the 1970s, which focused narrowly on humans' negative impacts on natural systems, sustainability seeks a balanced use of economic, social and environmental resources. This distinction means that an equitable use of resources can be achieved, while still providing profits to individuals and businesses. It makes the theoretical basis for sustainability more realistic and its outputs more useful than many of those produced by the environmental movement. As sustainability gains momentum, an interest in broadly connecting ethics and values with professional outputs has emerged.

This relationship between personal values and professional practice has inspired a new type of designer, one who is a strategic thinker, a successful creative maker, and an experienced communicator driven by values-based decision making.

Managing design

Design gives businesses a competitive advantage and helps to connect audiences and consumers with information, products and services. In order to achieve the most successful outputs, the design process must be managed. Design management deals with the coordination of resources, processes and people, so that objectives are met and the best possible outcome is achieved. Despite the fact that designers work in diverse situations and contexts, nearly all design projects will require management during their creation and production.

Successfully managing a design problem requires careful planning and implementation, as well as the ability to be able to predict how resources can be used most efficiently. Design management usually utilizes a clear and replicable process by which problems can be approached and eventually solved. The identification and execution of these methods can help designers more easily arrive at positive outcomes and can demystify the design process for clients and stakeholders.

Historically, design management has primarily been concerned with leadership, strategy, personnel management and the effective use of resources. However, in recent years, managers are increasingly being expected to make decisions and steer projects toward solutions that match the underlying values of the companies they work for and the audiences they serve. Design practitioners now give equal weight to the needs of audiences and consumers, while still working to create commercially viable products for clients. Design management provides an effective entry point to shift from purely profit-driven motives to objectives that value sustainable resources and look to achieve broader societal benefits.

Being an agent of change

This book reveals how design has begun to alter the contemporary landscape and looks at the designer as change agent, as explorer and as transformer. It investigates how specific aspects of the design process and a set of targets, including materials, technology, storytelling, collaboration and partnerships, can yield sustainable profit-driven solutions. The aim of this book is to answer two of the most pertinent questions that face values-driven designers: what makes sustainable design, and how can design help to create a more equitable and environmentally sensitive future? The text highlights how companies and organizations approach values-driven design in different ways. Through examples, the book examines the common target areas that are pertinent to ethically minded designers. The text includes case studies that describe how leaders in the field are producing market-ready sustainable solutions, and informational sections that give readers necessary background on the topic.

This book is for designers who want to learn about values-driven design and effective business practices by thinking and by example. It will help beginners define sustainability and design management through the application of ideas and process. It will provide experts with possible collaborators and new ways of framing problems and creating solutions. The book is designed to accommodate readers with various needs and interests. You are invited to read from back to front, dip into sections that relate to a project you are working on, or flip through the text to find images that engage you.

SUSTAINABILITY,
THE ULTIMATE ARTFORM

**1 Sustainability:
The Ultimate Art Form**

This report cover uses origami, the Japanese art of paper folding, to illustrate the connection between efficiency and sustainability.

1.1 Estonian Pavilion

The Estonian Pavilion at
Shanghai EXPO 2010 was an
interactive space that focused
on topics related to growing
cities through community-based
initiatives, collaboration, and
networking. The space included
giant piggy banks of visitor's
ideas for making the world's
cities better and a screen
showing the world's best cities.

CHAPTER 01

The Basics of Sustainability and Design

Design adds value and gives physical or visual form to objects, content and ideas. It may provide an exterior spatial form to products, the visual face of a brand, or it can solve problems that users never even knew existed. Design is part art and part science, and as such, its practitioners are taught to work under multiple constraints.

The capability to work within a given set of parameters is combined with the ability to approach a problem even when there are no clearly defined outcomes. In such instances, a designer may work from a broader set of goals and objectives to create a strategy for successful solutions.

As one tries to understand the multifaceted ways that design can affect sustainability and values-based initiatives, it is helpful to define design broadly by its approach to problem solving rather than to focus on the different deliverables produced by practitioners.

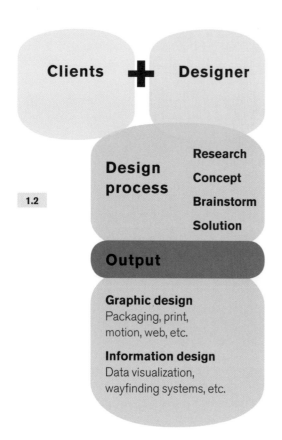

1.2

1.2 Design outputs

An articulated design process including research, concept development and brainstorming is used to produce a variety of visual and product-based solutions.

The role of designers

In its complex history, design has served many masters, often simultaneously. Design is an intermediary between client and producer, and between raw materials and the manufacturer. Some think that the role of designers is that of visual stylist or of making content understandable, attractive and easy to approach. Others see a more complicated role for designers, as complex problem solver, strategic thinker and as collaborator for businesses, non-profit organizations, entertainment and government sectors. In reality, design is all of these things and more. The role that designers can play in contemporary society is multifaceted.

Understanding how design can affect stages in the life cycle of products and the creation services provides an entry point for designers to make informed choices about how they produce products and services. Similarly, consulting and design management can be used to produce outputs that are more successful and expand the types of problems designers can work to solve.

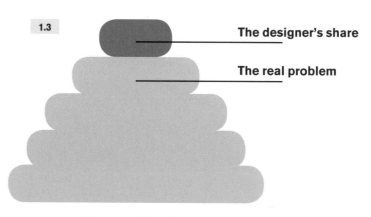

1.3

1.3 Papanek's idea of design

This diagram highlights the limited impact of design if the goals for projects are not increased to include a broad set of objectives.

Design as a hub

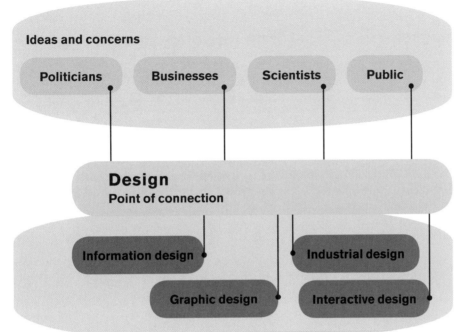

1.4 Design as a hub
Design often acts as an intermediary between end users and a variety of other interests. This gives designers the ability to connect the needs and goals of different constituents.

Ethics

Thanks to pioneers and philosophers of design, such as Victor Papanek (1923–98), designers are now taught to work for clients while retaining concern for the ethical ramifications their work may have on consumers and users. Today's designers are trained to understand the concerns of stakeholders and consumers while creating successful and market-ready interfaces, magazines, products and other outputs. They have to understand raw materials, content and space (virtual and physical), and they are trained to work within, rather than against, strict physical and conceptual parameters. How designers navigate the possibilities and contradictions in their work can provide specific opportunities to ignite change while growing their practice professionally.

The planet's resources

Depletion of the planet's resources is at an all-time high, but people's appetite for more 'stuff' is far from sated. The planet no longer seems capable of indefinitely sustaining human populations. In recent history, Western countries have benefitted most from industrial and post-industrial development.

Those of us who have gained the most from development, have the opportunity to be at the forefront of a movement to reduce and reverse the negative impact that industrial growth has had on our environment and social systems. It may seem that these are issues best dealt with by politicians and scientists, but design has an important role to play as well. Design can be used as a hub and as the point of connection between various interest groups. These groups can include, but are not limited to, public and government sectors, non-governmental organizations (NGOs), businesses and consumers.

What does 'capital' mean?
In this case, capital refers to anything that is input into a system, product, service or business venture.

Sustainability 101

Sustainability is commonly defined as the balanced use of social, environmental and economic capital, so as not to compromise the ability of future generations to survive and thrive. The key to understanding sustainability is to recognize the power of social, environmental and economic considerations working together. This combination is commonly referred to as the 'triple bottom line', or 'people, planet and profit'. Designers should be sensitive to the three prongs of the triple bottom line, but in one instance, working sustainably may focus more on the environmentally friendly production, while another output might stipulate that employees receive fair compensation and produce a product in safe and equitable conditions.

Therefore, as we consider what it will take to achieve true sustainability, we must strive for a holistic balance that respects the interdependent relationships characterizing both human needs and natural systems.

1.5

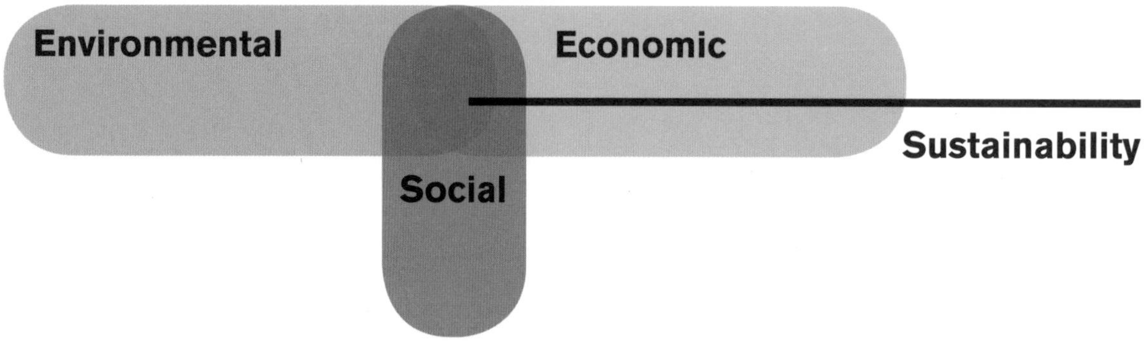

Environmental **Economic** **Social** **Sustainability**

1.5 Connection points
This diagram shows how sustainability can act as a connection point between the concerns of professionals from various disciplines and other stakeholders.

Natural systems

An easy way to understand the difference between the environmental movement and sustainability is to take the argument that we should safeguard natural systems all the way to their end point. For example, if the only goal were to preserve the environment, then the most effective, though extreme, solution would be to remove humans from the equation. It is generally agreed that the health of natural systems would improve tremendously. Obviously, that solution is incompatible with the needs of those of us already on the planet.

What is sustainable design?

In the face of so many variables, it is appropriate to ask: *what is sustainable design?* The answer is both nuanced and complex, but it can also be remarkably simple. One may approach sustainable practice with a focus on materials, by building communities, by changing the way users interact with products and services, or by focusing on use, reuse and recycling. However, it is not necessarily limited to these examples. Sustainability can mean so many different things that it challenges practitioners to be visionary, adaptable and innovative.

When practising sustainable design and thinking, designers should try to achieve systems that can exist indefinitely without sacrificing the needs of people and their environment. The case studies in this book illustrate how opportunities exist to create sustainability in the private and public sector, at work and in the community.

With so many ways that designers can choose to improve the output of the goods and services that they produce, a range of terms have cropped up to describe different focuses and ways of working. For example, *ethically minded* design simply means that we use our values and ethics as a gauge when producing work. In the case of *socially* or *environmentally conscious* design, these terms imply that there has been a focus on care for the environment and people's well-being. Since there are no exact criteria attached to these terms, they denote a spirit of working more than a specific set of rules.

When designing for the greater good, ideas are just as important as media and materials. But how designers actualize their understanding of sustainability can differ significantly depending on the type of design that they practise. By examining what the most forward-thinking designers and companies are doing today, it is possible to find clues that show how to apply sustainable thinking to solve common design problems.

Economic theories

For more on economic theories of sustainability, read *Natural Capitalism* **(Paul Hawken, Amory Lovins and L. Hunter Lovins, Bay Back Books, 2008);** *The Ecology of Commerce* **(Paul Hawken, HarperBusiness, 2010), and** *Green to Gold* **(Daniel C. Esty and Andrew Winston, Wiley, 2009).**

1.6 Charles Eames chair

Designed by Charles and Ray Eames, the Eames Lounge Chair was released in 1956 by the Herman Miller furniture company. Made of moulded plywood and leather, the chair is comfortable as well as stylish, and has become an iconic example of the principles of modernist design in practice.

1.6

History of managing design

During much of the first half of the twentieth century, design was an intensely stratified profession. In many studios low-level workers brought visual and three-dimensional form to the concepts originated by well-known and more experienced professionals. Where it existed, this cult of personality enabled famous designers to have enormous power over the creative process. For example, Charles Eames (1907–78) – famous for his furniture designs – demanded, and was given, complete creative freedom to work on a film for the 1959 American National Exhibition in Moscow. Several years later, he made use of a limitless budget to create IBM's exhibition *Mathematica: A World of Numbers. . . and Beyond*. Charles Eames, Paul Rand, Raymond Loewy and other twentieth-century luminaries, relied on fame and audacity as much as on talent, to convince a client that their designs were on the right track.

Paul Rand 1914–96

The American designer Paul Rand was famous for his international typographic style of graphic design. His work included logos for IBM, UPS and Next.

Raymond Loewy 1893–1986

Raymond Loewy was a French-born industrial designer who worked with many high-profile companies including Shell, BP and Coca-Cola.

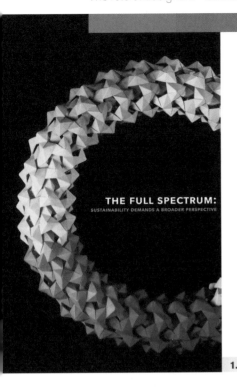

THE FULL SPECTRUM:
SUSTAINABILITY DEMANDS A BROADER PERSPECTIVE

1.7

1.7 Eco-friendly paper at NewPage

NewPage paper uses a 'full spectrum' approach to sustainability. In this promotional brochure, the designers have used colourful photographic imagery to complement information about the environmental performance of the company.

Designing collectively

While previous success can be a good indicator of the value of future work, since the 1980s, the pragmatics of the design process have evolved to focus less on one individual and more on a collective group of professionals who solve design problems using articulated steps and methodology. This change has given rise to the prevalence of successful design studios and agencies that rely on the cumulative creative enterprises of many equally talented designers. The role of managers, who deal specifically with the design process, is to steer the creative endeavours of workers and to interface with clients.

Unlike project managers, who mostly concern themselves with timelines and budgets, design managers coordinate a broader set of creative, budgetary and physical resources to ensure the successful outcome of stated objectives on behalf of clients. These leaders help clients to understand that design offers a competitive advantage, the ability for a company to differentiate and reposition itself, and can offer a direct means of communicating with an audience. In some instances, design management is the purview of a single individual while in other cases, the tasks associated with the methodology and implementation of creative ideas are divided between several people working together to steer a project and realize the successful outcome of a design problem.

At the small UK-based Elio Studio (see chapter 4, page 126), founder Leonora Oppenheim takes on both the role of project manager and creative director whereas at a larger agency, such as Mother New York, employees are divided into teams with one member overseeing specific projects and then reporting to a higher-level manager or creative director. While size is not the only determining factor for how management duties are delegated, it often plays a big part. Large firms tend to have more structured management frameworks and smaller companies or partnerships often gravitate towards looser systems.

1.8 Knoend

Knoend is a San Francisco-based design studio, operating on the belief that design can be a catalyst for change, with the power to create new experiences that will bring enhanced meaning to life. Knoend's founder, Ivy Chuang envisions how design can affect interaction between people and resources.
(Image courtesy of Knoend.)

1.8

Creating change

People have a tendency to think that change only happens at a macro level – big change, big companies and big government. While it is true that transitioning to more sustainable growth will require large changes, it is individuals whose combined impact has the power to change the world in its entirety. Talking to clients and encouraging them to adopt more environmentally responsible print production may seem like a drop in the ocean compared with the impact that a large Fortune 500 company has on the use of resources.

1.9

However, once a company truly buys into change it often opts to voluntarily increase its environmental performance not only in the short-term, but with long-range goals as well.

Paper companies

In the 1970s and the 1990s, environmental regulations in North America forced paper companies to change their production practices and reduce the pollutants produced during the paper-making process.

Companies such as Mohawk, Domtar and Neenah Paper not only embraced these changes, but also looked for specific ways to radically improve their environmental performance. Mohawk now uses clean energy to power its mill in upstate New York and has a zero landfill policy. Domtar works with the Forest Stewardship Council (see page 39) and has become a proponent of sustainable forestry practices; and Neenah uses the waste from its facility in Wisconsin to produce 'green steam' and a glass aggregate that is used in asphalt and roof shingles.

Each of these companies makes information about sustainable practices and consumer choices available on their websites and advocate for the adoption of environmental certifications (see page 38).

Employing sustainable design can help the consumer to navigate a world of confusing labelling systems and suspect products. It can reduce waste. It can help to incite political and social change, and it can involve overseeing the production of all a client's physical output.

1.9 Showcasing raw materials

It can be challenging to help consumers make the connection between raw materials, production and final products. This novel approach shows a sustainably managed forest with a large poster of the workers who are responsible for its maintenance and use. Photographic imagery helps viewers understand this paper company's commitment to responsible use of raw materials.

1.10

1.10 Continuity

The painting 'Continuity' by Cameroonian artist Idrissou Njoya illustrates the benefits of long-term partnerships.

Partnering with clients

Designers can begin by transforming their own work, exceeding their clients' expectations, and engaging with a public whose notion of sustainability ranges from ignorance to enthusiasm. Creating long-term relationships with clients provides opportunities to initiate an ongoing dialogue about a business's impact on its workers and natural systems; and at the same time, it helps to ensure the economic success of a designer or studio. Working repeatedly with the same clients can help guarantee a steady workflow for studios and designers; and building and maintaining relationships fosters trust.

Clients may not be ready to change practices overnight, but sometimes an analysis of a company's competitive position can provide data for a design team to make suggestions about adopting more environmentally friendly or socially sensitive practices. For example, if design managers identified a higher return on investment (ROI) for outputs that were aligned with customer values or showed how going beyond environmental regulations could safeguard against future costs, clients might consider changes in policy. Clients might also implement a pilot programme to test whether these ideas have monetary and environmental benefits.

Once companies include sustainability in their management agenda, almost none reverse the trend. Seventy per cent of managers interviewed for the MIT Sloan Management Review's 2011 Special Report on Sustainability say sustainability has 'a permanent place on the management agenda', and more than two-thirds say their organization's commitment to sustainability increased during the last year. Moreover, the report suggests that companies with a strong commitment to sustainability are more likely to look for partners and collaborators who can help them to achieve their objectives.

As designers look to manage client expectations and embed design thinking into business practices, they can look for context-specific ways to communicate how sustainable practices can improve their client's economic outlook and help to drive innovation.

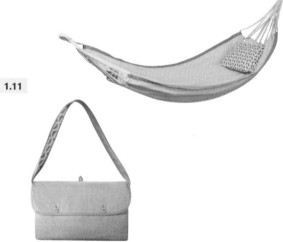

1.11

1.11 MIO for Target
MIO's product pitch for Target, the large American retailer, included a hammock made of organic cotton with bamboo buttons that folds into its own bag.

'Designing the artefact is meaningless unless you can create the conditions for its success.'
Valerie Casey, designer

19

Envisioning solutions

Designers are being called upon to envision a future rather than to simply respond to the needs of the present. As a result, graduate students at MIT Media Lab (US) and Royal College of Art (UK) create prototypes for products that respond to human needs or specific conditions but are not yet, nor may ever be, marketable. These concept products have been featured in exhibitions in New York, such as at Cooper-Hewitt's *Why Design Now?* and the Museum of Modern Art's 2011 exhibition, *Talk to Me: Design and the Communication Between People and Objects*.

At times the 'real' cost of a product over its entire life cycle (from materials extraction to disposal) is the most important area to focus on and there are designers who now specialize in 'life cycle assessment'. Other designers work on creating products that curtail consumption or help consumers make healthier food choices. For example, *GOOD* magazine uses infographics to make complex information and ideas visually accessible. Their 'What's Wrong With Our Food System' graphic was produced in partnership with Oxfam Australia and highlights how food producers can still be among the one billion people who go to bed hungry.

1.12

SUPPORTED BY

GREENING WESTERN QUEENS FUND OF **NORTH STAR FUND**

1.12 Promoting energy efficiency

The Greening Western Queens Fund invests in energy-efficiency and environmental projects in the Western Queens, New York, a community affected by widespread power outages in 2006. For the poster, designer Noah Scalin created an illustration that showcases recognizable parts of the city, while highlighting growth and regeneration.

1.13

Innovative solutions

There are as many solutions to producing sustainable outputs as there are designers trying to achieve them. An important way to understand how to apply sustainable concepts to design projects is to look at innovative work. Leaders in sustainability are helping to develop new materials and technical applications. They are using storytelling to connect consumers with context and relevance for the products that they buy. They are also creating information graphics to help audiences understand the difference between real and perceived needs.

1.13 Designer as activist

The 2012 Richmond Vegetarian Festival (US) used cut paper to illustrate the festival's mascot, a cow, juggling vegetables. Noah Scalin founded Another Limited Rebellion, and is an activist for social and environmental issues. In addition to running a successful design studio, Scalin writes about how designers can produce socially and environmentally sensitive work on his blog and in *The Design Activist's Handbook* (Noah Scalin and Michelle Taute, HOW Books, 2012).

Motivators driving business

Companies are motivated by a broad set of inputs. Competitive and financial concerns may be primary drivers in many situations but, as described in subsequent chapters, brand recognition and altruistic goals can also inspire business strategy. Similarly, positive and negative external factors stemming from government policies, economic variables and even media coverage can influence decisions. While design-related methodologies cannot completely mitigate or overshadow these internal and external forces, they can provide additional means of developing effective strategies to respond to market forces, generate revenue and respond to the social and environmental concerns expressed by stakeholders.

Avoidance versus investment

It would be an oversimplification to say that Europe and Japan rely more on regulation whereas the US looks to business-driven solutions for environmental problems. However, the reality is that many businesses dislike state intervention and, complemented by a litigious reflex, this makes the implementation of new regulations extremely challenging for governments. In the US, industry-based lawsuits and lobbying by special interest groups have lead to a near standstill, if not degradation, of environmental laws, with companies claiming that new regulations will hurt the economy, kill jobs and drive them out of business. This automatic reaction against regulation can be traced to a cultural avoidance and a fear of change that characterize the internal culture of many corporations.

Interface Inc.

Ray Anderson, CEO of the world's biggest carpet manufacture, Interface Inc., an early adopter of voluntary sustainable practices, has been one of the most vocal advocates from within industry. At a meeting of fellow executives at North Carolina State University (US), Anderson famously asked the audience whether he knew them well enough to call them 'fellow plunderers'. He went on to outline the pillage and plunder mentality that characterizes most industries and to challenge his audience to join him in looking for alternatives. While acknowledging that no company is 100 per cent sustainable today, Anderson has set a goal for Interface Inc. to become a sustainable company by the year 2020. In Anderson's case, a personal epiphany motivated him to re-evaluate his business practices; however, a shift can come from extreme adversity as well.

1.14

1.14 Car charging station
Simple iconography is used to indicate the location of an electric car charging station. An increase in fully electric vehicles is likely to necessitate new signage systems to help owners find charging stations.

The car industry

In 2008, the economic meltdown brought on by faulty mortgages led to the near collapse of the US auto industry. Injections of billions of dollars of capital by the US and Canadian governments provided a much needed lifeline for General Motors (GM) and Chrysler. As a result, in 2011, GM was able to begin promoting hybrid and electric vehicles, showing that the newly reorganized company sought to become a leader in fuel efficiency. In the US, home charging stations are being promoted at Lowe's Home Improvement stores in the suburbs of major metropolitan areas.

In the UK and Europe, companies such as Nissan and BMW also sell electric cars. Some governments provide financial incentives to encourage buyers to purchase electric cars. The increased interest in fuel efficient and more environmentally friendly vehicles has less to do with advances in technology (hybrids have been available for more than a decade) than it does in an evolution in consumer thinking and pure practicality. The rate at which American consumers purchased vehicles rated more than 30 miles per gallon more than doubled between 2011 and 2012, and brands like the SMART and Fiat, initially popular in Europe, are now selling in the US as well.

1.15 Electric cars
A variety of battery-powered plug-in cars are currently available and some manufacturers are already exploring technology that would allow electric vehicles to charge using non-cord based systems.

23

Using design thinking to solve problems

General Motors (GM) and Chrysler responded to severe market pressures and Ray Anderson had a personal vision. However, there needs to be a more systematic and predictable method to help organizations make the shift towards sustainable practices. In a 2006 article in *Fast Company*, industrial designer Mark Dziersk recalls how Allen Samuels, a professor and dean at the University of Michigan, told him and fellow students that any profession could benefit from design. Dziersk goes on to describe design as a process of doing rather than a product or end result. He connects this idea to the methodology known as 'design thinking', which he defines as 'proven and repeatable problem-solving protocol that any business or profession can employ to achieve extraordinary results'. Similarly, Roger Martin, dean of the Rotman School of Management at the University of Toronto (Canada) is interested in how design thinking can be broadly applied to business situations.

In his book, *The Design of Business: Why Design Thinking is the Next Competitive Advantage* (Harvard Business School Press, 2009), Martin details how design thinking was used to transform the company Procter & Gamble, and goes on to highlight other instances of its use in organizational management. There are indications that frameworks initiating in design disciplines are increasingly being deployed to solve a diverse range of problems. And, with its ability to identify positive outcomes without necessarily having clear goals at the start, design thinking can be seen as a conduit to help businesses embrace innovation and re-imagine the relationship that they have with social and natural resources.

1.16

1.16 Hybrid electric vehicles
With the introduction of the Prius, Toyota became a pioneer in hybrid vehicle technology. The car's design included an innovative touch screen with an energy use and fuel efficiency monitor.

Activity: Electric vehicles

In 1998, the 100 per cent electric GM EV1 (electric vehicle) was introduced for lease in select American markets. The company ended up recalling all the vehicles under a maelstrom of publicity that is chronicled in the 2006 documentary film, *Who Killed the Electric Car?*

01	View the film *Who Killed the Electric Car?* with a partner or in a small group.
02	Research the current market for hybrid and electric cars, focusing on Toyota's Prius as well as newer offerings from North American, European and Asian manufacturers.
03	Compare and contrast the political and cultural context in which the EV1 was launched versus today's markets. What is different today?
04	List the top three challenges you see with the integration of 100 per cent electric vehicles.
05	Identify five ways that design might help overcome those challenges. Write down your answers and collaborate with a classmate or co-worker to discuss your proposal. Can you convince your partner (or group) that design can make a difference?

Expanding the role of designers

The term 'design consultant' refers to a broad set of professionals who identify strategy, manage internal and external resources and create design outputs. A growing number of creative agencies and design studios now list 'consulting' among their offerings. IDEO refers to itself as a 'design and innovation consulting firm'. Its competitor, frog, similarly positions itself as a leader in innovation rather than a traditional product design studio. This evolution reflects a broader change in the industry, which seeks to place design thinking alongside innovation and strategy as core competencies for designers.

Design consultant

The design consultant, whether a sole designer or part of an embedded team, can help to define a competitive strategy, manage uncertainty, organize resources and position design correctly in the context in which a business operates. Many creative organizations see values-driven design as an obvious extension of their mandate. This allows design companies and individual consultants to more broadly define their outputs and expand the range of clients that they work with.

frog, whose Project Masiluleke is featured in chapter 5 (page 138), has a company-wide directive to design for positive social impact and seeks partnerships and clients who can further those goals. No longer are captains of industry the coveted source of income. Now, governments, non-profit organizations and educational institutions are employing design services in new and unusual ways, and motivating designers to expand the types of service that they offer to clients.

1.17

1.17 The Noun Project
The Noun Project is a global visual language of icons that facilitates communication regardless of geographies and without the need for text or translation.

The Designers Accord

In 2007, Valerie Casey, formerly of IDEO, frog and Pentagram, founded the Designers Accord, a 'global coalition of designers, educators and business leaders working together to create positive environmental and social impact'. To adhere to the Designers Accord, design firms, corporations and educational institutions adopt five guidelines that deal with the integration of sustainability into their core business practices. Since establishing the Designers Accord, Casey has broadened her personal mandate to include working with large companies and internationally based organizations. She challenges designers to take a global perspective and to become more involved with solving less defined and more complicated problems. In her role as design consultant, Casey works as part of a multidisciplinary team, which often focuses on broader strategies rather than traditional design deliverables.

Casey is a proponent of engaging with, rather than demonizing, corporations and argues that large multinational companies have the influence, economic resources and global footprint to make tremendous change possible. Without their cooperation, she says, 'We will never be able to advance any meaningful social missions'. Casey believes corporations have come to understand the fragility of the marketplace, see constant change as the new normal, and are looking for meaningful ways to have a positive impact on the environment and consumers.

The idea of forming allegiances with multinational corporations makes some people uncomfortable. However, Casey and other proponents of this type of engagement such as Adam Werbach, a former Sierra Club president and Chief Sustainability Officer at Saatchi & Saatchi, point out that the scale of the impact can be achieved with such partnerships are far greater than those realized by individual designers or even inspired entrepreneurs.

Guidelines for design firm adopters of the Designers Accord

1 Publicly declare participation in the Designers Accord.

2 Initiate a dialogue about environmental and social impact and sustainable alternatives with each and every client. Rework client contracts to favour environmentally and socially responsible design and work processes. Provide strategic and material alternatives for sustainable design.

3 Undertake a programme to educate your teams about sustainability and sustainable design.

4 Consider your ethical footprint. Understand the environmental impact of your firm, and work to measure, manage and reduce it on an annual basis.

5 Advance the understanding of environmental and social issues from a design perspective by actively contributing to the communal knowledge base for sustainable design.

Guidelines for corporate adopters of the Designers Accord

1 Publicly declare participation in the Designers Accord.

2 Provide strategic and material alternatives for sustainable design of products and services, and pledge to help customers reduce their negative impact.

3 Undertake a programme to educate your teams about sustainability and sustainable design.

4 Consider your ethical footprint. Understand the environmental impact of your organization and work to measure, manage and reduce it on an annual basis.

5 Advance the understanding of environmental and social issues from a design perspective by actively contributing to the communal knowledge base for sustainable design.

1.18

1.18 Wooden 'Terra' bench
Architect, artist and furniture designer Maya Lin used FSC-certified red maple from Maine (US) forests to create a bench that highlights the beauty of an individual tree and a forest's terrain through its wave-like appearance.

1.19 Responsible production
Bowls like the one below from Bambeco can be produced using sustainable woods and safe dyes.

1.19

Best practice

The phrase 'best practice' is often used when describing sustainable outputs or production and yet it is not a concrete term that can be used to express a specific set of standards or objectives. Instead, it is a pragmatic way of referring to production and business practices that attempt to choose the best environmental and social options for the moment. Technology, processes and materials constantly evolve and what is considered best practice today may be merely passé in five years.

Constant improvement

The concept of best practice provides a useful launching point when designers are working to help clients to transition their internal processes and/or production standards. The idea of constant improvement is particularly appropriate for inclusion in a broadly defined strategy that may have to respond to market pressures or changing contexts during its implementation. Helping clients to understand the need for evolving objectives that may need periodic revision, can highlight the importance of incremental change as a necessary part of the journey towards more sustainable practices.

Given the fluidity of the market and ongoing improvements in systems and ways of working, this book does not try to quantify a perfect set of standards. Instead, it encourages designers and the organizations that they work with to investigate a range of materials and processes and adopt those that most closely fit their level of commitment and production requirements.

1.20

Pricing problems

Cost is one of the most common reasons why consumers fail to buy environmentally and socially responsible products. In a market-driven economy, volume of sales determines both the success of a company and the impact their practices will have on the environment and on social systems. In some cases, eco-friendly items actually cost more to produce, but to many consumers it can seem that anything labelled as eco-friendly or sustainable comes with a price premium. The perceived 'up-charge' for environmentally or socially preferable products can make it seem like there is an eco-tax associated with buying them, even though they do not necessarily cost more to produce. The confusion caused by pricing can be frustrating to cost-conscious consumers who want to make better purchasing decisions.

The *de facto* eco-tax or 'up-charge' associated with environmentally friendly products highlights several failings of the market and its current pricing and production structure. Some companies are simply cashing in on the trendiness of eco-friendly products and are hoping that consumers will continue to pay more for these items. These practices are deceptive and hurtful to the industry as a whole. Additionally, the supply chain system rewards companies that are able to produce items on a massive scale.

For example, the buying power of large retail chains such as Walmart, Tesco and Lidl is considerably greater than that of small independent stores.

The lack of clarity around pricing puts environmentally and socially preferable products and services out of reach for large portions of the population and causes other consumers to simply opt out. In chapter 2 (page 62) Susan Aplin, CEO of Bambeco, a retailer of eco-friendly home products, relates how her company is working to reduce 'green price inflation'. Aplin is working with her vendors to create a scalable system in her supply chain so she, too, can reach more shoppers with lower-priced items.

Designing for less

As designers, it is important to keep cost in mind and to design products and services that do not have inflated prices simply because they are labelled as sustainable, eco-friendly or are produced using fair trade practices. Designers can work to reduce costs by specifying the most efficient production, creating new applications for recycled materials, embracing advances in technology and working with distributors to help bring prices down.

1.20 Nature as communicator

Patterns and textures from nature can be used to enhance visual interest or communicate specific information. Here Elio Studio has used imagery of ancient plants as biomimetic inspiration.

Touch points

A number of key areas can be defined as 'touch points' or 'targets' for environmentally and socially conscious designers. Most often used in tandem, these touch points provide a structure for identifying and examining solutions, while breaking down processes into steps that can be replicated. Most importantly, they can be used as a way to evaluate how social and environmental change is being implemented. During the strategy phase of a project it can be particularly useful to create a list of applicable touch points and assess how the specificity of problem, context and audience may dictate which areas can be targeted to produce a successful outcome.

In some cases, a lead designer or manager may share a target list with the client at the early stages of a project. At other times, it may be more useful for the design team to work through various possibilities and only share those that are relevant. As you read the following chapters and case studies, try to pick out which of the following touch points have been targeted in each example given. Then imagine how you would choose to affect change and create sustainable solutions given similar challenges.

Collaboration

Bringing professionals together from many disciplines can increase the likelihood that a team fully understands the problem and has the expertise to create meaningful and long-lasting solutions. Collaboration also provides opportunities to work on a diverse set of projects and in different geographic locations, and serve a broad range of clients.

Consumption

May refer to products or services that reduce the number of objects a person must own, or can refer to the development of longer-lasting products. Some designers suggest we need fewer, but better-designed objects in our lives and are creating products to fill that niche.

Efficiency

One of the most powerful and easy to apply targets of sustainability, efficiency is often overlooked. It is something that every organization should strive for and an area where one improvement is usually possible. Reducing the amount of energy used in production and/or specifying processes or vendors that use renewable energy is one of the most common ways to achieve greater efficiency.

Entrepreneurship

In addition to working for clients or as part of a larger team, many designers with expertise in sustainability are creating their own companies with the goal of delivering exemplary products and services. Entrepreneurs may start a new business or work to bring a product or service to market using existing distribution channels.

Fair trade

Fair trade (see glossary) is a market-based approach that seeks to help producers and workers attain fair wages and equitable working conditions. Fair trade organizations can connect socially conscious designers with producers. Creating opportunities for workers who have previously been exploited to earn fair wages provides benefits for both workers and consumers.

Innovation

Describes the introduction of a new idea, service, device or product. Innovation may require the development of processes or even machinery that is used to make objects and create sustainable deliverables. In some cases, a completely new output or service may be the product of design innovation.

Materials

The sources of raw materials, their method of extraction from the natural environment and their transportation to manufacturing facilities can all be substantial improvements. Additionally, designers should try to use fewer raw materials and specify those that eliminate or reduce toxicity in a product's life cycle. Concern for materials should also include the health of people living near extraction or recovery sites.

New markets

Identifying or creating new markets is an excellent way for designers to create positive links between production and consumption. The use of new markets is particularly dynamic when working in the developing world and trying to find outputs or solutions that can benefit local communities.

Problem solving

Often linked to innovation, problem solving examines the ways a designer may approach a problem by redefining the solution or even rethinking the brief. In this area, a designer may come up with a completely new product or service, or redefine how an existing product is used or manufactured.

Production

How an object is manufactured and the various inputs and outputs of production is a key area to focus on to improve the environmental performance of a product. This area may require the designer to switch vendors and/or alter their designs so that preferable processes can be used in production. It is important to consider the physical health associated with working in a manufacturing facility.

Reuse/Recycling

One of the biggest problems we face is an over-abundance of waste. A key area to focus on is the use, reuse and recycling of materials that would otherwise be discarded. Ideally, we should design within a closed-loop system thereby transforming waste into useable materials. This target may include making items that are designed to be disassembled, reused, recycled or composted, or designing products that are made from recycled or reused material.

Storytelling

Storytelling connects an audience with information. At its core, storytelling provides context and relevance about a product, service or company. It is an undervalued, but important touch point for sustainable designers.

Strategy

Design strategy focuses on successful problem definition and planning rather than traditional visual and object orientated outputs. Strategists may be part of a larger design team or they may be brought in as consultants to help steer larger projects and help define successful outcomes.

Technology

Technology may include improvements to systems, manufacturing and production equipment, and may require the adoption of new systems or processes as well as initial capital investment.

Collaboration

Consumption

Efficiency

Entrepreneurship

Fair trade

Innovation

Materials

New markets

Problem solving

Production

Reuse/Recycling

Storytelling

Strategy

Technology

Case study
SHAGAL | iodaa

Efficiency

Innovation

Materials

Problem solving

Production

Reuse/Recycling

Storytelling

Technology

Who SHAGAL | iodaa, an interdisciplinary office for design, architecture and art

What Design research and outputs addressing the issues that result from unchecked growth

Where Zurich, Switzerland

Why it matters

SHAGAL | iodaa (see www.shagal-iodaa. net) illustrates how consulting and traditional design practice can be combined to create a successful studio. Founded by designer Dr Lui Galati and architect Dr Siamak G Shahneshin, their work addresses issues resulting from unchecked growth, such as land use and spatial and economic organization, in both self-initiated and client-based projects. Shahneshin and Galati act as the studio's directors and draw together arts- and science-minded designers to work on projects from the broadest possible perspective.

Creating questions

SHAGAL | iodaa seeks to reframe contemporary approaches to design by working with a multidisciplinary collaborative methodology. Shahneshin explains that their process consists of a strategic dialogue-based system that includes clients, architects, artists, graphic designers, engineers, industrial designers, landscape architects and manufacturers who work together to create built environments that speak to contemporary and future users.

The SHAGAL | iodaa team is wide ranging both in its members' expertise and their geographic and cultural origins. Their strength comes from that collective knowledge. Rather than having a dedicated arm of the studio specializing in environmentally responsible design, SHAGAL | iodaa creates solutions for public and private-sector clients holistically. The output produced by them does not always match conventional expectations of designed deliverables. As consultants, they may produce plans, positive future scenarios or may work on planning and strategy.

1.21–1.22 Business cards

Business cards created using sustainable green technology.

1.23   **1.24**

1.23–1.24 Dubai Trilithons

A vertical paradise within the Middle East is designed to be a metaphorical vertical bridge connecting the three largest world religions. In addition to promoting peace, the towers would be an example of Dubai's environmental stewardship. One hundred per cent of leftover concrete is collected from demolished buildings in Dubai .

1.25

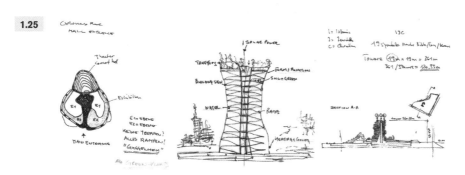

1.25 Preliminary sketches

Preliminary sketches for the Dubai Trilithons.

The importance of research

Much of SHAGAL | iodaa's output takes the form of research and planning. For designers who are obsessively focused on the physical production of objects, this may seem to be a bit unusual. Not every designer wants to spend the balance of his or her time thinking rather than making. But new areas of specialization – including research and strategy – have given rise to professionals who may never produce physical objects or visually style design deliverables. For SHAGAL | iodaa's designers, ideas and understanding are just as important as any other tool. Research has been an integral part of the studio since its beginnings. To those who doubt that cerebral endeavours are as important as physical output, Shahneshin praises the benefits of research.

Shahneshin does not believe that companies working alone can achieve significant environmental improvements. 'Togetherness is key', he says. It is inevitable that many current interdisciplinary practices will become tomorrow's best practices, but Shahneshin cautions that, 'many of today's innovative solutions may not be able to sustain future challenges'.

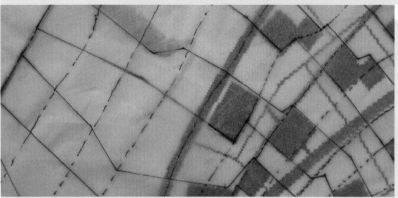

1.26

1.26 Urban-Fabric-Recycling
SHAGAL's plan for a compact urban area is based
on medieval city planning and includes conditions,
forms and site that generate new urban structures.

1.27

1.27 Open space
Instead of suburban-like sprawl, open space
is built into a denser city space and urban structures
are generated by the existing elements particular
to the site.

*'Working sustainably is
ganz-einfach (so simple/
so ordinary). How can
a designer not work
sustainably?'*
Dr Siamak Shahneshin,
sustainable designer

Reframing problems

As an interdisciplinary collective practice,
SHAGAL | iodaa is set up as a meeting of the
minds and seeks to capitalize on the strengths
that professionals from different backgrounds
can bring to problem solving. The company
works on a range of projects, but its goal is
to help bring about solutions with a multifold
increase in eco-effectiveness. If that seems
like a tall order, Shahneshin concedes that, in
some cases, this type of far-reaching change
will require improvements to current production
techniques that have not yet been developed. In
Shahneshin's opinion, the way to achieve these
improvements is to put an emphasis on both
creative problem solving and opportunity seeking.
This reframing of problems into opportunities
is a methodology that SHAGAL | iodaa has
begun to implement. 'Focus close to home first',
Shahneshin says. 'The most fundamental tool
is self-consciousness and self-examination.
Through self-assessment we may discover
the blueprints for carbon neutrality and green
sustainability.'

Many of the issues that currently seem urgent
have been discussed in some form since the
1970s. But today, Shahneshin still sees a political
landscape with enormous concern, but too
little action and too few solutions. Whether one
takes a theoretical or more practical approach,
Shahneshin believes in the urgent need for
issues to be translated into an actionable
agenda for the design profession. When asked
about the difficulty of getting new systems and
ideas adopted by governments and businesses,
Shahneshin points to his own history of difficulty
and disappointment. In the early 1990s, he
developed a plan for free bike lending for
downtown Milan (Italy) only to have it rejected
because it did not have monetary benefit for
the city. Years later, a similar programme was
adopted in Zurich (and other cities). While change
may not always come as quickly as Shahneshin
would like, he sees improvement and, therefore,
continues to focus on pushing green sustainable
design through innovation.

1.28

1.28 Bike sharing
Bike sharing has been
adopted by Zurich,
Switzerland.

Activism and strategy

By working as advocates and activists, SHAGAL | iodaa designers have campaigned for green tax relief and have helped to create strategies for transit subsidies and low-income transit passes. Visual output is also part of the studio's output, and it has produced posters, specialized paper bags and egg baskets, all with the goal of dematerializing and using economy of means.

Shahneshin is beginning to see more recognition for the vital role that green sustainable design can play in the environment, and the financial, social and psychological well-being of humans. In the end, he believes it is the job of the designer to dream and to make those dreams a reality. The challenge, he says, is time. He recalls a New York gallery whose slogan was, 'Time is always now'. 'Whenever I hesitate, I think of that slogan', Shahneshin says. 'Let's not lose our time. This is our call.'

Activity: Design for the greater good

The following questions provide a starting point for thinking about design for the greater good. After answering the questions, make notes and create an outline that includes your interests and the ways they could connect with causes or promote preferable production practices and the choice of materials.

01	What are you working on today?
02	Is it sustainable? Can it be sustainable? Or are there ways to shift what you do in order to work on values-based projects?
03	What target areas could you focus on and where can you see the most immediate opportunities for improvement?
04	Given your current design practice, what are the challenges of working sustainably today and in the future?
05	How can these challenges be overcome?

2.1 Non-traditional media

UK-based CURB delivers a client's message using unusual and non-traditional media. This chalk advert is eco-friendly and is unique because of its scale.

CHAPTER 02

Strategies

By properly framing and understanding the scope of design problems, designers can imagine and create innovative opportunities for products and ways of meeting customer needs. Tools originally intended for use in business management and marketing can been applied to design-specific problems as well. These methodologies provide a useful means for strategists, managers and designers to assess the strength of internal and external resources associated with a project or company, and for evaluating whether a given plan or a set of objectives is likely to succeed within a specific context.

'Good design is a quantifiable benefit, not just a cost.
Its value can be measured economically, socially and environmentally.'
British Design Council

Terminology and branding

Labelling can present challenges, both in the correct use of terminology and in its applicability to branding and market positioning. There are a dizzying array of 'socially and environmentally preferable' labels attached to products, businesses and even design services (often in an effort to increase market share and profitability). These markers can be an indicator of underlying values or the attributes of a particular product; but in some cases, they are vague and can even be misleading. In countries where the use of terminology is unregulated, oversight often comes from consumer groups, and in some places, advertisers may be able to promote the environmentally preferable features of a product without proving those claims.

In order for design outputs to be successful and to achieve relevance, the benefits and shortcomings of values-based labelling, and the regulations that may govern the use of these terms, need to be analysed. After careful consideration of a brand's market position and target audience, it should be possible to recognize when it is appropriate and/or legal to publicly identify with a specific cause and use environmentally or socially relevant terms.

Unclear labelling

A variety of terms have arisen in popular speech and business marketing to describe socially and environmentally preferable products. Unfortunately, unclear definitions and mislabelling often cause concern for consumers who may not understand how they should evaluate products with these attributes. In most of the world, the use of the term 'green' is unregulated and poorly defined. Still, 'green' is everywhere. It pervades our consumer and media culture.

It is used to advertise products and is linked to marketing campaigns and government initiatives. With everything from cosmetics and cleaning products to coal and SUVs labelled 'green', it is troubling that the term does not denote any specific features even though the public's perception of it is generally positive.

When clearly labelled and truthfully marketed, there is nothing intrinsically wrong with products using the terms 'green' or 'eco'. But these terms, and their benefits, are limited unless they are backed up by certifications or regulatory systems such as the European Union Ecolabel (which legislates how agricultural products and foods stuffs can be labelled).

Certification

In location or market sectors where the use of terminology is not regulated by governments or other entities, independent third-party certifications are the most reliable way for manufacturers and customers to make responsible purchasing decisions. Certifications such as International Organization for Standardization (ISO see page 97), fair trade certifications (see page 119) and the European Union's Eco-Management and Audit Scheme (EMAS) ensure that products are measured equally against a set of rigorous standards.

Certifiers make information about how materials and production processes are evaluated, available to the public and often encourage the use of a mark or visual symbol to show that a product has achieved the relevant standards.

2.2

The Green Movement

The Green Movement is a political and social ideology seeking to promote the importance of the environment, sustainable management of resources and social liberalism through changes in public policy and individual behaviour. With its origins in the 1970s, the modern Green Movement takes different forms depending on location and the aims of various groups, organizations or political parties.

2.2 Reusable shopping bags

These reusable shopping bags designed by the Florence-based studio Frush use a handmade stencil to feature the client's logo. Frush works to produce successful design, sustainably.

2.3

2.4

2.5

EMAS

The European Union Eco-Management and Audit Scheme (EMAS) is a management tool for companies and other organizations to evaluate, report, and improve their environmental performance (see www.ec.europa.eu/environment/emas).

2.3 EU Ecolabel

EU Ecolabel is a voluntary label promoting environmental excellence that is recognized throughout Europe. The Ecolabel helps consumers to identify products and services that have a reduced environmental impact throughout their life cycle, from the extraction of raw material through to production, use and disposal (see www.ecolabel.eu).

2.4 The Green e-logo

The Green e-logo identifies products made by companies that purchase certified renewable energy to offset a portion or all of their electricity use. Renewable energy types include, but are not limited to, wind power, solar power, low impact hydropower, and biomass (see www.green-e.org).

2.5 Forest Stewardship Council (FSC)

FSC is a non-profit international organization established to promote the responsible management of the world's forests. Products carrying the FSC label are independently certified to assure consumers that they come from forests that are managed to meet the social, economic and ecological needs of present and future generations (see www.fsc.org).

2.6

Make decisions that consider the amount of resources the world offers.

Be aware of the materials that you are using.

Recycle, buy environmentally friendly products and use public transport.

When environmental and social consensus meet economics, it's not just best for your wallet or the environment but also for the lasting impact it has on society.

Preserve the earth by not being wasteful and recycling.

Recycle and compost piles.

Be aware of nature and conserve all that it has to give us.

Being green is about respecting the earth.

Windmills and solar panels.

Perceptions of sustainability being green

= Sustainability

= Being green

2.6 Perceptions of sustainability being green

People's perceptions about sustainability versus 'being green' can differ considerably. When working to achieve sustainability, it is important to consider each aspect of the triple bottom line, i.e. people, planet and profits.

Sustainable services

If you decide to offer sustainable services, there may be an opportunity to build that information into the 'about your organization' area, if there is not a separate section on corporate social and/or environmental responsibility.

Identifying with eco terminology

In some cases, it is inappropriate for a business to be branded as being sustainable. Also, not everyone wants to be identified so specifically with a defined set of values or an environmental mandate. Sometimes, this may be because they are afraid of alienating existing clients or because a large segment of work is done in a sector that is hesitant to be linked with what is largely perceived as an environmental movement. Understandably, many designers want to focus more on the core services that they provide and believe it is important to emphasize their skills, such as creating great products and communicating information and ideas. Designers do not have to brand themselves as 'sustainable' 'green', or 'eco,' to work for the greater good.

Large companies and design firms, for example, may choose to embed environmentally or socially sensitive services into their existing offerings without changing their overall brand image. In 2011, 67 per cent of managers interviewed for MIT Sloan Management Review's Special Report on Sustainability said that pursuing sustainability-related strategies is necessary to be competitive and another 22 per cent stated it would be in the future. Not all of those companies will actively identify with a sustainable agenda, but they may brand certain products as 'eco friendly' or offer customers more information about their environmental performance through corporate social responsibility (CSR) reports. Being truthful and transparent is still the most important consideration in branding. Do what you say you do, and do it to the best of your ability. Using overtly sustainable messaging to talk to clients is secondary.

2.7

Is pursuing sustainability-related strategies necessary to be competitive?

↗ Yes

87%

55%

↘ No, but will be in the future

22%

32%

↘ No

7%

8%

2.7 MIT Sloan Management review and The Boston Consulting Group

Most of the managers interviewed for the MIT Sloan Management Special Report on Sustainability believe a sustainable strategy is necessary to be competitive. Many also say they are 'deriving financial benefit from these activities' and that sustainability is driving innovation within their companies.

= 2011
= 2010

2.8

2.8 ECODE product labelling

ECODE is a prototype labelling system that began as a student project. Its aim is to provide a clear, consistent graphic code for eco-labelling.

CSR reports

Corporate Social Responsibility (CSR) reports (also called sustainability or environmental reports) began to be used about two decades ago as a way for companies to make information about their environmental performance available to shareholders and the public. CSR reports also include information about the social impacts of companies' practices including labour relations, worker rights, and the use of systems such as fair trade. CSR reports are not legally regulated. However, the Global Reporting Initiative (GRI) has created the most widely used guidelines for sustainability reporting and many companies use its standards as a framework for content, disclosure and for measuring improvements.

2.9

unmundofeliz.org

is the mediterranean sea a life's sanctuary?

Greenwashing

Greenwashing is the unsubstantiated claim of better environmental performance by a company or individual service. It is both dangerous (depending on the context) and unethical, and puts the entire market at risk. Unfortunately, even if greenwashing occurs, it does not necessarily mean that a regulatory agency will begin an investigation or that there is any way of substantiating the claim made by a company about its brand. Consumers are not necessarily looking for perfection, but they are definitely looking for honesty.

Greenwashing endangers not only those who participate in this unsavoury practice, but also the long-term success of companies who are doing their best to honestly report their progress and performance. The difficulty comes when consumers cannot tell the difference between the truth and the hype. In such cases, audiences may suffer from green fatigue and abandon environmental performance as a basis for their decision-making.

2.9 Clear messages
Simple visuals of the outline of a whale with a heart for a tail and an 'x' where the eye should be communicate the message for this campaign against animal torture and abuse.

Transparency

Transparency is the best way to ensure that consumers are not confused by mixed or misleading messages. Clear messaging can be as easy as describing what the company is doing today and outlining where it hopes to go in the future. Invite feedback and suggestions. Some of the best ideas for innovation may come from the people who use a company's product.

A closed-loop system

The ultimate goal of sustainable products and services is they exist in a closed-loop system. This means taking into account end-of-life issues, materials sourcing and production. In some cases, bringing a product to market in a timely way may mean that not all of these issues are addressed as well as one would like, but that does not mean that one should not talk about the goals for how the company wants to improve its environmental and social performance in the future.

Values-based branding

Values and ethics play an important role in branding both for designers and the companies they work for. A company's brand can convey and support the ideology of that organization across a wide range of media. Consistent communication works to reinforce the power and visibility of the brand within a given market. Incorporating sustainable values into mission statements and corporate charters is a good way to start, but communication materials should continue to inform and educate consumers while providing a clear and consistent voice. Many consumers want products and companies that are aligned with their own social and ethical values, and strong design can help bring a visual presence to those values.

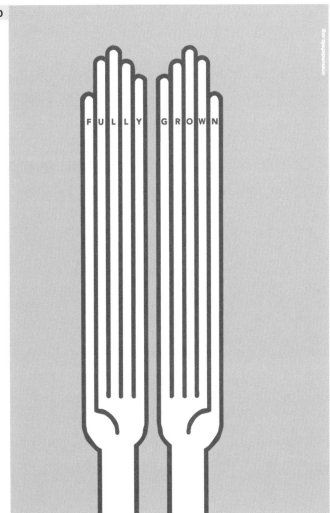

2.10

2.10 Connecting humans and nature

In Fully Grown images of elongated hands are used to communicate the idea of the relationship between humans and nature. Type takes a subordinate role and the use of the colour underscores the message.

2.11 GoodGuide

GoodGuide provides expert ratings on safety, health and environmental performance for food, personal care products, household chemicals and electronics. Information is available online and via the organization's mobile app (see www. goodguide.com).

The design audit

A design audit is a tool for reviewing design outputs and measuring how effectively design is used within an organization. It evaluates how well design deliverables meet the goals of the organization and match the brand's values and visual tone. A consultancy or external reviewer usually carries out a design audit. However, in some cases an internal team may conduct an audit as well. The benefit of working with a consultant is that they are less likely to be influenced by internal politics, and are more likely to be objective. However, in-house audits are typically less expensive and are a good option in situations where cost is a primary concern. Creating a working group with members of different teams or divisions can help mitigate problems with subjectivity that sometimes arise with internal audits.

The audit usually begins by collecting the objects or representations of the brand in various materials including identity marks, websites, brochures, catalogues, packaging, product design and advertising. A review should include the evaluation of the visual consistency of a brand, looking at the various materials produced, assessing whether they correctly target their intended audience, and deciding whether the visual and written tone match the company's vision and mission.

A design audit may show inconsistences in visual language and could highlight communications materials or products that are off message or incorrectly target an audience. In some instances, an audit may reveal new opportunities for design and can be used to show how design can enhance the output of an organization or play a greater role in meeting its long-term objectives.

The information found during a design audit is usually compiled in a report and may include a visual presentation. Results can be used to help define strategy, produce a set of recommendations for changes in future positioning, and identify opportunities for expanding the role that design plays within a company. In the case of a visual design audit (for graphic design) the data may be compiled into a manual, which highlights proper ways of using identifiers, typefaces, imagery and other visual material. While not traditionally part of design audits, information about the environmental ramifications of materials, such as paper, plastics and composites, can also be included. Additionally, evaluations of production processes and end-of-life issues can also be conducted and may be paired with a more complete life cycle analysis.

Shortcuts to better products and services

Establishing clarity in the messages and labels used by the retail market is an ongoing challenge, but in recent years sites like the GoodGuide (see www.goodguide.com) and Topten (see www.topten.info) have provided shortcuts for consumers concerned with transparency and greenwashing. These sites help to level the playing field by conducting an independent assessment of products, and are proving popular with consumers.

Topten operates in Europe and is a consumer-oriented online search tool that evaluates the best appliances in various categories. Its key criteria are energy efficiency, environmental impact, health and quality of the organization. Topten has established 'Best of Europe', which identifies the most energy-efficient products, stating the countries where they are marketed. Topten is working with partners to bring advocacy and reporting to other countries including the US and China.

In the US, political reluctance to enact sweeping climate reform legislation is part of the regular news cycle. It is hard to imagine Topten's original model, which includes funding from governments and EU agencies, being successful in the US and other regulation-resistant countries. Fortunately, rather than have a one-size-fits-all approach, the company encourage those who are interested in expanding Topten in other countries to customize the system to fit the specific needs of their location.

Rating systems for materials

While not as prevalent as consumer rating systems, there are tools and shortcuts that designers can use to evaluate materials. Paper calculators are free and available on most of the large paper company's websites. They allow graphic designers to calculate savings of trees and energy based on specific products and manufacturing criteria. For product designers and materials engineers, Autodesk® (see www.autodesk.com) has developed the Sustainable Materials Assistant® for its Inventor® software. Sustainable Materials Assistant helps manufacturers and designers to make responsible choices in order to reduce their environmental impact. The software is a database of materials and specifications allowing the user to estimate a product's carbon footprint and find out whether a material contains toxic or recyclable materials.

Working with like-minded organizations

One benefit of being identified as a sustainable company is that it opens doors to working with like-minded organizations. Socially- and environmentally-conscious companies are often more inclined to work with designers that share their values.

In some cases, being a sustainable company may provide opportunities for free training offered by government agencies on how to run an environmentally friendly office. In other cases, designers can join listing services where other sustainable organizations can search for vendors to work with. Designers are finding that aligning their values with the information they have about services can provide opportunities for collaboration and can be both personally and professionally rewarding.

2.12

Design thinking

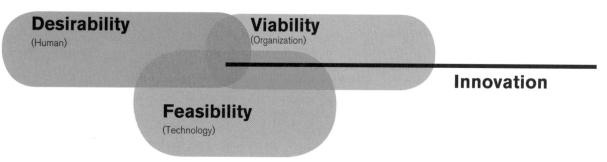

Desirability
(Human)

Viability
(Organization)

Innovation

Feasibility
(Technology)

2.12 Design thinking
Innovation can be found at
the intersection of desirability,
viability and feasibility. Each of
these attributes must be fulfilled
for a design to be successful.

The importance of strategy

Strategy is a plan of action designed to achieve a vision or set of goals and objectives. Every design project incorporates strategy to some degree. In some instances, strategy may be arrived at as part of a defined process of analysis, while at other times, strategy will be embedded in the more organic structure of design thinking.
A design strategist usually collaborates with a team, which may include the client, designers with diverse specializations, as well as marketers, ethnographers and business professionals.

The ways in which design thinking can be applied to non-design problems are diverse. When looking to create a design-specific strategy, it is useful to begin by asking: what can design bring to bear on a problem, situation or on resources? Tim Brown, CEO of IDEO and author of *Change by Design*, writes that: 'Design thinking offers an approach to innovation that is powerful, broadly accessible and can be integrated into all aspects of business and society.'

Whether working from a brief or in a less defined situation, Brown believes that designers must work within the practical constraints of business and the allotted resources. He describes the limiting factors on design as feasibility, viability and desirability. How a design solution responds to these variables will differ, but to achieve success, a product must be feasible to produce, viable from a cost and distribution standpoint, and desirable to the consumer.

Creating opportunities for design

By identifying where design fits within an organization, it is possible to connect sustainably and ethically driven outputs to real market needs. Strategy provides a framework for designers to achieve linkages that can identify and respond to new opportunities while meeting business objectives. Design solutions and strategy should always complement a company's existing vision, policies and the reality of the market. Developing an effective strategy can begin with a series of questions:

- What are the core values of a company?

- Who does it serve, or for whom does it produce products?

- How will those products benefit the users or consumers?

- How can the capacities of a company be harnessed to create future success?

- What role does design play in the brand and for the consumers/audience?

Design strategy

If a company does not have an articulated design process, a design strategist or manager can look at the current structure of the organization and work to implement design methodology that complements existing functions, personnel and processes. It is important to determine what role design will play in larger institutional objectives and assess whether the design outputs are meeting those goals. If it is found that the context or competitive market has changed, realignment will be needed. The brand and/or design solutions should be repositioned according to changes in trends, company objectives, needs and audience preferences.

A strategist's outputs may include a detailed analysis of a problem (with or without proposed solutions) or series of objectives and achievable goals. What is produced will depend on the nature of the organization or client, the scope of the project and the context in which outputs will exist. In addition to understanding the objectives of a problem, a strategist will discover measures for success and help identify the stakeholders who should be part of the problem-solving process. Technical parameters, budgetary guidelines, organizational requirements and time constraints are often evaluated and may be defined as part of a strategy.

To develop objectives, one should begin by analysing the mission and vision of a company. Mission is why the company exists and what it plans to achieve. Vision refers to how an organization sees itself and what makes it different. In the short term, design can create value for both organizations and consumers.

Some organizations have positioned themselves as 'corporate citizens' and strive to match their values to their consumer base, and may even let their consumer base dictate or influence how they produce products.

For instance, Patagonia founder Yvon Chouinard was an early proponent of sustainable practices in business. Online, Patagonia's products and environmentalism are given equal billing (for more information see www.patagonia.com). Consumers can join the Common Threads Initiative – Patagonia has a variety of this type of programme – which encourages customers to use products for as long as possible and to reuse or recycle redundant items. Patagonia is able to connect to like-minded consumers and to advocate for change. In such cases, a strategy based on specific environmental or social values can be an important tool to aid in brand differentiation, and for identifying ways in which design outputs can be used to solve existing problems and realize unmet needs.

2.13 MIT Sloan Management Review and The Boston Consulting Group

The internal and external drivers of sustainable business practices as reported to researchers at the MIT Sloan Management Review by 4,000 managers from 113 countries. In 2011, 41 per cent of respondents listed customers' preference for sustainable products and services as the reason for changing business practices.

2.13

Which of the following factors have led to changes in your business model as a result of sustainability considerations?

Percentage	Factor
41%	Customers prefer sustainable products/services
35%	Legislative/political pressure
30%	Resource scarcity (e.g. increased commodity prices and price volatility)
28%	Competitors increasing commitment to sustainability
26%	Stricter requirements from partners along the value chain
25%	Owners' demands for broader value creation (i.e. more than profits)
23%	Competing for new talent
20%	Customers will pay a premium for sustainable offering
19%	Meeting demands of existing employees
16%	Maintaining 'license to operate'

Steps for developing a design strategy

2.14

Consider	
Mission	What we do
Vision	Who we want to be
	Audience and competitive analysis
	Unmet needs
Review	Internal and external factors impacting design
Create	Goals and objectives
Evaluate	What is ideal? What is most important? What is realistic in a given time frame and with available resources?
Develop	An actionable plan for implementation and synthesize into appropriate output

2.14 Mapping strategy
Following defined steps for developing strategy can help ensure consistent and successful results.

Design strategy should:

- Be aligned with the client's/company's mission and brand values.

- Position the client/company in a distinct or unique way against competitors.

- Put the brand/product in a position of trust with audience/consumers.

- Create actionable objectives with a clear plan for implementation.

Use design strategy to:

- Plan how design elements can be used to meet existing business goals.

- Create a plan of action that leads to a design solution.

- Help position a client more effectively in their competitive landscape.

- Transition objectives into a guiding focus for design related work.

- Translate brand vision/mission into actionable design-related goals and objectives.

- Help steer decision making.

- Focus a brand or client towards social and environmentally responsible outputs.

- Align design deliverables with the lifestyle and ethical values of the client or consumer.

2.15

Threat of new entrants.

Bargaining power of suppliers.

Rivalry among existing competitors.

Bargaining power of buyers.

Threat of substitute products or services.

2.15 The five forces that shape industry competition

1. Threat of new entrants.
2. Bargaining power of suppliers.
3. Bargaining power of buyers.
4. Threat of substitute products or services.
5. Rivalry among existing competitors.

Five competitive forces

'Five Competitive Forces' is a system for evaluating competitive positioning that was originally outlined by Michael E. Porter in a 1979 article in the *Harvard Business Review*. Porter wrote about the five forces that shape competition and influence the profitability of an industry or company. He suggested that even though industries may appear to be very different, the same underlying forces affected their profitability. Depending on the industry and market factors, there will be continuous flux in how the forces can influence a company. When considered together, Porter's five forces can be used to help determine long-term profitability and to develop an effective business strategy.

Porter's model is largely predicated on the notion that there is a plentiful supply of cheap labour and it puts no value on environmental resources. Values-based companies and designers who look to reduce the impact of goods and services on the environment may be uncomfortable with the purely profit-driven model. Fortunately, environmental economists, such as Paul Hawken and Amory Lovins, have developed theories suggesting that respecting the environment and being socially responsible can increase a company's profitability. This model may be better for values-driven businesses.

Natural Capitalism

The book *Natural Capitalism: Creating the Next Industrial Revolution* by Paul Hawken, Amory Lovins and L. Hunter Lovins, (Little Brown and Company, 1999) includes tangible examples to show how businesses can thrive while achieving a balance between life and commerce. The authors suggest that a new phase of industrialism has begun, which is characterized by the loss of living systems, emerging scarcity and the need to begin valuing natural capital. To enable people, governments and businesses to value all capital, including natural capital, Hawken and the Lovins suggest the implementation of four strategies:

1 Radical resource productivity: slows resource depletion, lowers pollution and provides a basis to increase worldwide employment with meaningful jobs.

2 Biomimicry: reduces wasteful output of materials and can be accomplished by redesigning industrial systems along biological lines.

3 Service and flow economy: is based on the flow of economic services that can better protect the ecosystem services upon which it depends.

4 Investing in natural capital: works to reverse worldwide planetary destruction through reinvestments in sustaining, restoring and expanding stocks of natural capital.

Research

Research is an important step in most design projects, but it is an integral part of design strategy. Without the insight gained from research, strategy may target the wrong audience, or overlook solutions or processes that have previously been attempted. Research is used to gain insight into an audience, understand the contextual environment in which an output will exist, compare a client's business to its competition, and evaluate the likelihood of success. The material gathered during the research phase of a process takes many forms and may include periodicals, professional and academic journals, white papers, scholarly or journalistic writing, evaluations of government pressures and regulation, field research and data gathered from test groups.

Three categories are used to describe particular characteristics of research material and the ways in which it is produced. Primary research uses data that is collected in real-world situations and may allow the researcher to engage with users to help solve problems and discover unmet needs. Primary research is a mainstay of 'user-centred design.'

Secondary research includes the summarization and synthesis of data that has already been collected and may include dictionary and encyclopedia entries, journal articles, magazine and newspaper articles, as well as criticism or commentary.

Tertiary research uses data that has been distilled and collected from primary and secondary sources. Reference books, almanacs, manuals, textbooks, chronologies and indices are all examples of tertiary research. Primary and secondary research are commonly used together to provide a multifaceted picture of a subject.

Benchmarking

Benchmarking is used to establish a competitive baseline and compare what one company is doing against other firms in the same area. It can also be used to test how the current design holds up against the competition and to understand why particular firms may be successful. To begin with, the best companies within the same or related sector are identified, and their processes and results are compared against one's own, or those of a client. When used to evaluate design outputs, benchmarking may include putting existing designs, products or preliminary explorations side by side with those produced by competitors and evaluating their similarities and differences.

It is preferable to conduct benchmarking exercises at the beginning of a project before a lot of time has been spent coming up with fully realized design solutions. Then the data gained from comparison exercises can be applied to new design iterations. Benchmarking is a good way to assess why successful companies perform well. However, it is important to take that knowledge and use it to create original innovative solutions rather than mimicking what has already been done. This will ensure that one's own company or client is continually working to be an innovator within a given market.

Activity: Benchmarking

Use the benchmarking techniques to assess the strengths and weaknesses of a popular brand (it is not absolutely necessary to chose an eco-friendly or socially conscious company). Design materials from the brand or company you pick should be easily accessible either online, as visual representations or in physical form.

Part A: Research

01	Identify a company to focus on for this exercise.
02	Briefly list what the company sells, its target market and the name of at least three competitors (if you aren't able to list three competitors, go back to step 01 and choose a different brand).
03	Begin collecting design materials that are representational of the company's brand. You can find actual products and collateral materials or you can use existing photos or advertisements. Remember to include digital manifestations of the brand (e.g. websites, mobile sites or banner ads) as well as physical objects, such as catalogues and advertisements.
04	Do the same for each of the three competitors.
05	Using a large work surface or wall, lay out all the materials for each of the companies. If you need to present your findings to others, it is helpful to attach materials to separate boards.

Part B: Analysis

06	Using the materials gathered for Part A, note the positive and negative attributes of various design solutions.
07	Compare the subject brand to its primary competitors and determine which company uses design most effectively. Make a list of positive and negative ways each competitor uses design compared with your subject company.
08	Based on the list from Step 07, determine five or more changes the subject company could use to make more effective branding or product development. Consider the target audience (see Understanding the audience page 54) and whether there are unrealized opportunities for design to positively affect the value and public image of the brand.
09	Present these findings to your group or class and discuss the possible challenges your proposals might face and whether or not it is likely that your subject brand would actually be able to implement your solutions.

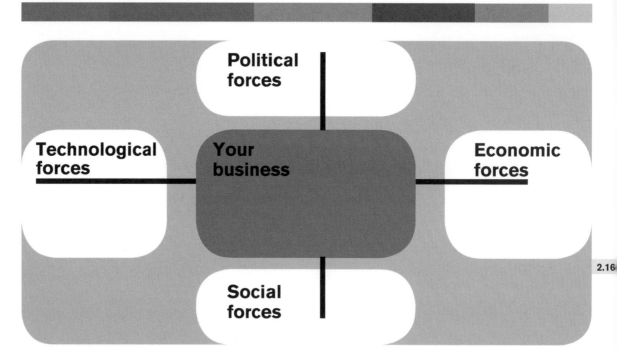

Tools for business analysis

Internal and external forces can affect the function of an organization. They can help to determine growth and decline and can affect the outcome of initiatives. A variety of tools have been developed to analyse these factors and aid in business and strategic planning. Several of the most common frameworks can be combined to provide an accurate picture of the causes that influence success or failure and may be used to evaluate particular proposals or courses of action. A PEST (Political, Economic, Social and Technical) analysis is most often used in conjunction with a SWOT matrix (Strengths, Weaknesses, Opportunities and Threats) and Porter's Five Competitive Forces evaluation system (see page 49). These tools should be used to assess the strengths and weaknesses of an organization, to determine the effectiveness of current competitive positioning, and to explore the viability of strategic initiatives.

2.16 PEST

Understanding how Political, Economic, Social and Technological forces affect a business can help managers to develop realistic strategies for product development, pricing, placement and promotions.

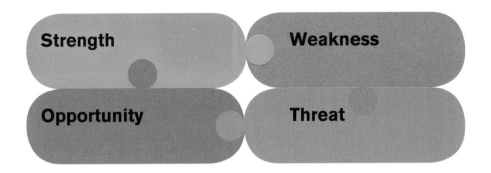

Strength

Weakness

Opportunity

Threat

2.17

PEST (Political, Economic, Social and Technical)

PEST analysis requires one to define relevant political, economic, social and technical factors affecting a company or business environment, to gather data or information about what affects these factors and, finally, to synthesize the information into useful conclusions. Sometimes environmental and legal variables are assessed separately (known as a PESTEL analysis), while in other instances these indicators are included as aspects of the original themes.

PEST is most useful when one needs to analyse the macroeconomic factors affecting a business. The information produced may inform branding, marketing and design, as well as overall business management. Which factors have the most effect on a company depends on the goods being produced and the geographic and political environment. For example, a company that produces consumer electronics might be most concerned with technological factors, such as research and development (R&D), materials sourcing and manufacturing; and economic factors, including interest rates and economic growth. Whereas an organization with an educational mission might be influenced more by social conditions, such as population growth and age distribution, and political factors.

SWOT (Strengths, Weaknesses, Opportunities and Threats)

A SWOT matrix is a decision-making tool that helps analyse strengths and weaknesses against opportunities and threats, and can be used in strategy development and planning. It allows users to identify opportunities that fit the particular attributes of an organization and the competitive environment. SWOT can be used in workshop settings or brainstorming meetings and is a good framework for assessing strategy, position and marketing of an organization.

Although there is some overlap between PEST and SWOT, PEST is usually used before rather than after SWOT, since SWOT can be used to assess a particular business proposition, plan or set of objectives. PEST is used to more broadly evaluate the market and competitive positioning.

Understanding the audience

Evaluating the values, habits, likes and dislikes of consumers can form the basis for design development and increase the likelihood that design deliverables correctly target the audience. An audience analysis helps to determine how a product or brand can connect to a need in consumers' lives, what resonates with them, what their concerns are and what motivates their behaviours. Marketers, designers and ethnographers, working internally or as hired consultants, usually conduct this type of research.

Since it is unlikely a company will see a return on investment by targeting low-return consumers, an audience analysis most often tries to identify which people will have the greatest value and what may motivate their behaviour. This allows a design team to create original content targeted to high-return consumers. When conducting an audience analysis, it is usually best to use a combination of demographic and psychographic information. Demographic information is concerned with factual elements such as age, gender, location, personal wealth and race; whereas psychographic data looks at how people make decisions and what is meaningful to them (including motivators, lifestyle, beliefs and values).

Psychographic research focuses on subjective information and may include questionnaires, surveys and focus groups. When creating an audience profile it is useful to identify who will be targeted (demographic data), why a person may buy a product (psychographic data) and what aspects of that person's life or values may affect his or her purchasing decisions (ethnographic data).

Demographics

Demographics can be used to produce an objective profile of a person or a group of similar people. In design, demographic information is often used to produce an audience profile. Categories to look at include:

- Gender
- Age
- Race
- Ethnicity
- Education level
- Marital status
- Income
- Employment
- Home owner or renter
- Type of products purchased
- Amount spent on specific product categories

Psychographics

Psychographic research is used to define a person's motivation for behaviours including buying habits, special interests, lifestyle choices and their goals and aspirations. Psychographic research is useful because it helps designers and marketers understand why consumers behave a certain way. The data collected can be used to classify consumers according to their aspirations, opinions and lifestyle choices. Conducting psychographic research can be expensive and it is sometimes criticized for producing data that is not objective. This type of research is best used in conjunction with other information gathering methods.

Values and Lifestyle categories (VALS)

In 1978, the Stanford Research Institute (SRI) developed a system for psychographic categorization called VALS (Values and Lifestyles) that can be used to separate people into eight clearly defined types. This market segmentation is used to help companies understand what will most likely appeal to their consumers and to differentiate their buying patterns. VALS has been updated several times since its creation. It is important to note that people may move from one level to another as they age and that factors such as marriage and having children may affect their needs and preferences.

Ethnography

Ethnography is a field of study where research is usually conducted through first-hand observation of behaviour and may be used to gain understanding of a person's values and decision-making (often related to culture and/ or ethnicity, religion etc.). In the past, ethnography was primarily conducted by anthropologists and sociologists, however, designers now participate in this type of research as well. When describing the role ethnography plays in design, The American Institute of Graphic Arts (AIGA) says: 'Designers need to understand the relationship between what they produce and the meaning their product has for others. They need to observe the people they are designing for in their own environments.'

AIGA collaborated with Cheskin, a strategic consulting and market research company, to produce a primer introducing the crucial role that ethnography plays in design (for more information see www.aiga.org/ ethnography-primer).

The VALS system

The VALS system categorizes people in several ways. Individuals are separated into innovators (thought to have high resources and high innovation) or survivors (low resources and low innovation). People are then further grouped into the following categories according to ideas, achievement and self-expression.

Ideas:
- Thinkers
- Believers

Achievement:
- Achievers
- Strivers

Self-expression:
- Experiencers
- Makers

2.18

2.19

2.18–2.19 Clean advertising
CURB uses natural materials such as stones, chalk and grass to create site-specific representations of a brand.

Development versus implementation

The development of strategy requires analysis, vision and communication, whereas implementation makes use of more traditional project management skills and planning. Once a successful strategy has been created, it should be implemented using an actionable plan. Resources and the roles of various people all need to be taken into account. Depending on the situation, implementation may be highly structured and can use systems such as the 'Responsibility Assignment Matrix' (see page 124), but realizing strategy can also be part of a more organic process. How fully a plan is mapped out ahead of time will depend on the size of the organization, the number of people working on a project and the context in which objectives need to be met.

While working in a timely fashion and on budget should always be the goals, it is important that a plan is not so cumbersome that it gets in the way of creativity, or includes so much red tape that implementation is delayed. What tools are used to make strategy visible will vary depending on the objectives for the project and the output that is being created. One should always strive to create a unique message or product through a combination of form and function. Rather than evaluating initial designs based on what is most appealing visually, search for the solution that solves the problem and meets all objectives as part of the overall strategy.

2.20

2.20 Amy Fox

Amy Fox is vice-president of innovation at Hyland's Inc., which makes safe and natural homeopathic remedies.

Interview: Amy Fox

Can you briefly describe your current position and responsibilities?

Currently, I am focused on growth through new product innovations and stimulating new growth for existing brands or products through design and messaging. These responsibilities include looking for market opportunities, watching trends, listening to consumer needs and working with teams to meet these needs in the form of new products, or updating the look of existing products.

What value does design bring to the industry in which you work? Where is design placed in the organization where you work?

Good design is critical, particularly when it comes to consumer product goods. The industry as a whole shows a variety of levels of commitment to design. I think this is in part because even some poorly designed products still meet a need and function for the consumer. The consumer is driven by function first, and then design. This hierarchy shifts slightly if the product is carried by or has an element of fashion that consumers feel would affect how people perceive them.

How have you been able to incorporate design into business strategy?

As a small company, we have to take the long view in this integration. Design has been an important part of our growth and our ability to communicate with the user.

What is the relationship between design and innovation?

Innovation can be interpreted in many ways. While innovation can create big leaps forward, often it can be reapplying or combining tried and true technologies in new ways that creates value. Design has an important part to play in both types of innovation.

How have you been able to use innovation and design thinking to help shape the brand of the company you work for and to target new markets and consumers?

This consumer-centric bias that we use both in innovation and design efforts teaches us about how to better connect with our current consumers, and we often find new ones. It is refreshing for us to see the validation in this process.

Is it important for a design manager to have any background in business?

I have both backgrounds, starting my career in design and then learning the language of business. I think design managers and designers are well served by understanding business. It helps you to realize the needs of the consumer and the client.

Are there any tools, methodologies or theories that you use or recommend to connect design with strategy?

There are basic business assessment tools. Most commonly referenced in this case would be Porter's Five Competitive Forces (see page 49) or a SWOT analysis (see page 53). The thing to remember about strategy and analysis is that nothing is ever static.

Case study
MIO

Who Independent design studio

What Sustainable products
for the home and office

Where Philadelphia, Pennsylvania, US

Why it matters

MIO is pioneering the use of
transparency in product information
to develop responsible product
experiences for the future.

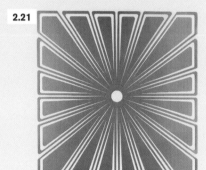

2.21

2.22

2.21–2.22 Bendant lamp

The Bendant lamp is a flat-packed
chandelier composed of a series of
leaf-like shades surrounding a central
fixture. You can bend the shades up or
down to create unique light and shadow
arrangements.

Green design for everyone

In 2001, when Jaime and Isaac Salm opened
MIO (see www.mioculture.com), green
was just a colour, and retailers were not
concerned with the environmental factors
associated with the design and production
of the goods they sold. More than a decade
later, MIO has found a niche as a design and
consultancy company dedicated to making
products that serve real needs today, while
introducing and developing responsible
product experiences for tomorrow.

MIO designs and produces lighting fixtures
made from wool, decorative wall surfaces
created out of recycled paper, side
tables inspired by origami, and countless
accessories that help consumers become
more organized. While product design is the
most visible output from MIO, the company
does not want to be defined as a 'maker
of objects'. Instead, MIO sees itself as the
producer of 'innovative design experiences'.
The designers at MIO also work with various
organizations and companies to produce
sustainable outputs through the consulting
arm of the company, CultureLab.

An overarching philosophy is a huge part
of how the company presents itself to
customers, particularly through its website.
Under the heading 'Philosophy', MIO
uses its online presence to pledge to use
materials that can be easily recycled using
existing infrastructures, fit into closed-loop
manufacturing systems, or fit seamlessly with
natural ecosystems.

2.23

2.23 Origami side table

The table is designed to get maximum use of standard metal sheet goods. The design eliminates unnecessary cutting and waste. Once bent, the table's folds lock the parts into place. The table includes recycled content, is recyclable, and has an environmentally preferable finish.

Carrots not sticks

As a designer and owner of a company that puts its values first, Jaime is concerned by the prevalence of marketing and advertising of green goods and services that uses fear, guilt and finger wagging. He suggests that 'carrots, not sticks, are the way to convince consumers they should vote for a better life with their currency'. Jaime believes we need to get people excited by making better sustainable products. Additionally, they should have greater flexibility, be better designed and improve efficiency. Jaime says: 'Sustainable goods should not be purchased because they are environmentally or socially preferable, they should be purchased because people love them.'

The MIO philosophy highlights the relationship between context and relevance and underscores the importance of a 'connection' between designers and their audience. Jaime maintains that nothing is developed in a vacuum: 'Even though we tend to think that technologies or behaviours occur spontaneously, in reality, they are the result of the context in which they happen.' Jaime says the products they design at MIO are all 'a response to our life, behaviour and social and political fabric of our time.' He believes this should be true regardless of whether one is designing sustainable products or not.

The products people buy and the ways that we consume energy and other commodities result in damage to the planet, to animals and to natural systems. Many of the products people use are only affordable because of inequitable wages and poor conditions for the people who produce them. For MIO's founders, design has a special role to play in the search for a more sustainable way of life, expressly because changing the inputs of people's consumption and production of products can be an effective response to the very real threat to our survival and way of life.

Simply put, Jaime says: 'Design that does not account for the environmental or social changes that we face is out of touch with reality'. He would like eco-awareness to be defined by where a product comes from and where it fits into society and our ecosystem, but he also believes that the social and cultural implications of a product should be addressed. 'The more we know about what we purchase, the more connected we feel with what surrounds us,' he says. To that end, each product that MIO produces comes with a description, a philosophy and information about the environmental ramifications associated with manufacturing the product.

2.24

2.24 Naked Line
Inspired to make honest and simple fashion, furniture pieces in MIO's Naked Line reveal the sustainable materials that most furniture makers try to hide.

2.25

2.25 Custom cabinet
Made from 100 per cent pre-consumer waste wood (formaldehyde-free particle board), this piece has sturdy sliding doors and back panels made from powder-coated steel.

Shorthand for customers

MIO uses a quick guide to the environmental and social attributes of its products, which is listed with the product description. For example, the Naked Line large cabinet and storage systems are labelled as 'renewable + recycled content + recyclable + environmentally preferable finish', whereas the Capsule light is 'renewable + recyclable + compostable'. For customers shopping on the MIO website, this is a noticeable distinction. Information about a product's environmental and social qualities, and where materials are sourced from is available alongside the measurements and product description.

The business perspective

Isaac Salm, who has a degree in Economics and Finance from the University of Miami, looks after MIO's finances and acts as the company's methodical guide. Isaac's business sense has proved invaluable because he can anticipate what the company will realistically have to overcome to make sustainable design successful in the marketplace. Isaac has a perspective on sustainability that designers would do well to heed. He believes sustainability should be a means to an end rather than an end by itself. Isaac thinks that both businesses and designers often look for a simple formula to add to their company or design practice. He says that is just not how sustainability works. 'There isn't a pill you can take to become sustainable,' Isaac says. 'Throughout the years, we have been able to grow a successful sustainable business because we have truly integrated sustainability into our business model.'

The holistic approach to everything from finance and marketing to operations and the social and cultural aspects of the business are integral to how MIO approaches every problem. Isaac recommends that designers begin by having a clear understanding of what their goals are, and then make sure that every decision and aspect of a project clearly accounts for the environmental, social and cultural aspects of the market that a project is targeting. He acknowledges it can be difficult to be mindful of so many touch points, but says that from his experience, 'the more you do it, the easier it gets'.

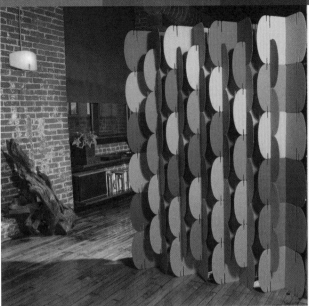

2.27

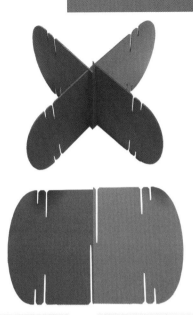

2.26

2.26–2.27 Nomad architectural system

Designed to grow and adapt to any environment and a range of applications, Nomad translates the tools of architecture into simple modules that anyone can use.

Made from recycled, double-wall cardboard, the system can be assembled into free-standing, sculptural screens, temporary partitions, even displays, without hardware, tools or damage to existing structures.

2.28

2.28 Composter

MIO's product pitch for Target (US) included a herb garden with a container made of 100 per cent post-consumer recycled paper, and a stylish home composter.

Consulting work

A substantial amount of MIO's business comes from its consulting work and from the work it does with large corporations. MIO has designed display systems for the clothing company Anthropologie; it has done consulting work for FedEx and pitched a line of products to the US retail giant, Target. Whether designing for their own product line or working for larger companies, Jaime and other MIO designers have a unified approach to problem solving. They begin with the understanding that problems are rooted in culture and in people's habits and behaviours. 'The objects are just a reflection of our preoccupations,' Jaime says. 'Sustainable design should be inspired and motivated by human behaviour and observations above all.' He emphasizes that we need to start adjusting behaviours, habits and cultures rather than just focusing on objects.

Like many designers and owners of businesses whose motives include ideals as well as profit, the Salms are realistic about the impact they are having on the planet. 'I do not believe that my products will change the world nor do I think that at the moment, our scale at MIO is significant enough to make a dent in the problem,' Jaime says. But they believe their products have changed many minds. They strive to inspire others to change by example and by energizing people with what is possible. By doing so, the brothers have had a real impact and created a collaborative environment that includes both the corporations they serve and their customers.

Case study
Bambeco

Consumption

Efficiency

Innovation

Materials

New markets

Problem solving

Production

Reuse/Recycling

Storytelling

Technology

Who Online retailer and distributor

What Fashionable, eco-friendly home products and accessories

Where Baltimore, Maryland, US

Why it matters

Bambeco combats green price inflation, or eco-tax, while helping to grow the market for eco-friendly products that will require a variety of designers to create them.

Eco-friendly products

Bambeco (see www.bambeco.com) is a retailer of eco-friendly home furnishings and interior products in the US. It pledges to combat what it sees as green price inflation and works with designers to internally develop at least 95 per cent of the products it sells. Bambeco president, Susan Aplin, a retail veteran with two decades of experience at Williams-Sonoma, Gap, Staples and Sports Authority, was inspired by seeing the ramifications of climate change while on a trip to Alaska.

Analysis showed that Aplin's carbon footprint was far better than the average American's, but she still wanted to find a more direct way to help reduce the negative impact that humans have on the planet and decided to put her experience in the retail industry to use, creating a brand that would focus on eco-friendly products.

2.29

2.29 Mango wood bowl

These one-of-a-kind bowls are made from mango wood. The mango tree bears fruit for 40 years. Then the farmer cuts it down to make room for new seedlings and local craftsman use the wood to produce beautifully simple bowls.

Calculate your carbon footprint

Numerous online tools are available for calculating your carbon footprint the way Aplin did. Some of these sites also sell offsets, while others simply provide raw data and/or information on how to reduce a person's carbon footprint.

Act on CO2 Calculator: www.carboncalculator.direct.gov.uk

Carbon Footprint: www.carbonfootprint.com

Terrapass: www.terrapass.com/carbon-footprint-calculator

WWF: www.footprint.wwf.org.uk

Customers are key

Every business caters to its customers, but Aplin says at Bambeco, 'It is all about the customers. If we are stumped about how to proceed or solve a problem, we take a step back. We pretend we are Bambeco's customers, and we ask, What would we want?' All companies should work toward sustainable business practices by producing the best products and services, but Aplin believes companies also have a responsibility to create change locally, nationally and globally. To that end, Bambeco works in the local Baltimore community to advocate for the benefits of a greener economy and has partnerships with international NGOs such as the World Wildlife Fund (WWF). The former mayor of Baltimore cited Bambeco's relocation to the area as an example of the economic benefit that can result from a city adopting favourable environmental policies.

Bambeco puts all current and future products through a 20-page evaluation that assesses the source of materials, manufacturing and production and examines the efficiency of shipping and distribution. The company is also working with NGOs and governments to put certifications in place where none yet exist. Bambeco's approach to growing a successful business and to transforming the industry is three-fold: the company focuses on design, the environmental and social integrity of its products and advocates for fair pricing.

Starting with great design

First and foremost, Bambeco works to create and sell high-quality products. This is vital in a sector where some consumers still have the impression that green products are lower quality. This is certainly a misperception, but Aplin feels that in her industry a person's perception is reality, so she emphasizes that quality and usefulness have to be the primary focus for designers whether they are creating sustainable products or not.

Cost issues

'We know what it costs to produce products and right now we see prices being artificially inflated,' Aplin says. She is all too conscious that green products need to be cost-effective to achieve full market penetration. Disrupting the current trend of inflating the cost of green goods will not only make Bambeco more competitive but, Aplin hopes, it will also force her competitors to adopt more honest and fair pricing policies. Bambeco's margins are healthy, so Aplin is confident that injecting a bit of pricing honesty into the industry will help move sustainably designed products into mainstream consumer outlets.

Aplin also disagrees with those who argue that sustainable products usually cost more to produce. 'Why would we ever have the impression it costs less to tear down a tree, transport it and produce a piece of furniture from the raw material than it costs to find and use reclaimed material, much of which happens to be close to distributors and retail outlets?' Aplin asks. She believes that what is currently missing in the industry is efficiency in the supply chain and the ability to scale production up to meet the demands of large retailers, both are areas on which Bambeco is focused.

2.30

2.30 Recycled glass bird feeders

Bambeco uses environmentally preferable materials whenever possible. These bird feeders are made from recycled glass and decorated by hand. The nectar basin attaches to the bottom with a recycled rubber stopper.

Storytelling

'There is an aesthetic you can only get with something that already has history to it,' Aplin says. She gives the example of tables made from reclaimed wood, which ship with photos of the original beams and production steps. It is such products, and the idea of reusing steel from train cogs, that gets the staff at Bambeco excited. But Aplin is quick to point out that while storytelling is important, not every environmentally preferable product has a sexy narrative attached to it, nor is every customer interested in why a product is better for the environment. When appropriate, Aplin and her team make information available to consumers, but she reminds customers that making a product and transporting it to consumers is equally important.

2.31

2.31 Outdoor mats

This sturdy outdoor mat is made with recycled rubber.

2.32

2.32 Natural or reused fibre
Some Bambeco rugs are crafted from recycled soda bottles, milk jugs and packaging materials while others are made of jute a natural sustainable fibre.

Opportunities abound

Aplin is confident that the market for eco-friendly products is strong. When asked to respond to the fear that some designers have about their ability to find jobs that allow them to do values-based work, Aplin's response is off-the-cuff and exuberant. 'Give them my number, and we'll be happy to hire them,' she says. Even though it may not be possible for Bambeco to absorb every designer who is looking to align their personal values with their professional output, Aplin's generosity and unbridled optimism are excellent indicators of how many opportunities exist for new designers to create positive change in the world.

Activity: Redefine a category

One way of increasing the number of environmentally preferable products available to consumers is to redefine a category. For example, two producers of cleaning products, Seventh Generation (see www.seventhgeneration.com) and Method (see www.methodproducts.co.uk), took two very different approaches to connecting eco-awareness with cleaning products. Seventh Generation actively advertises the environmental attributes of its products, whereas Method's sustainable values are less known. The company's R&D department works to develop less harmful ways of cleaning and packaging products, but Method's branding and marketing primarily focuses on creating appealing scents and attractive visual styling for packaging.

01	Using secondary research sources (see page 50) analyse Seventh Generation's and Method's branding strategies. Decide what makes each effective for the market and audience they are targeting.
02	Identify a product and/or category that could be redefined or that could benefit from the addition of a new environmentally friendly version of an existing product. Using psychographic and demographic data (see page 54), create a profile of the audience you would target with a new or redesigned product.
03	Create sketches of the new product and its packaging or create a print- and web-based advertising campaign for the product. Use the data collected during step 02 to inform decisions about which audience to target and what kind of visual language can be used to connect to those consumers.
04	Solicit input on the preliminary design from a classmate or colleague. Develop finished comps, layouts or renderings.
05	Create a multi-paged proposal using research gathered during steps 01 and 02 and the final designs developed for step 04. Lay out the pages in a program like Adobe InDesign to create a visually cohesive product to include in a portfolio or to show to prospective clients.

3.1 Responsability

Responsability by Cameroonian
artist Idrissou Njoya.

CHAPTER | **03**

Design Creating Change

When used responsibly and in the correct context, design can act as a powerful conduit for change. Physical enhancements or improvements, such as those developed by product designers or materials engineers, can literally alter the built landscape. Communication designers may use devices such as metaphor or analogy to connect audiences with messages designed to alter their thinking or improve their understanding of a social or environmental issue.

Even though practical and production-related issues often take centre stage in conversations about environmentally preferable products, a seismic shift in values will be required to achieve a balance between the needs of people and the environment. This transformation can be encouraged by thoughtful and sometimes persuasive public service announcements, location-specific interventions and the development of design solutions and policies that inspire more responsible consumption.

3.2

Design that deserves to exist

Practitioners looking to engage in values-driven design and to create sustainable outputs need to be concerned about more than fulfilling a client's objectives. As suggested elsewhere in this text, they have to ask whether or not the outputs they make deserve to exist in the first place. There are numerous examples of wasteful and unneeded design. Communication design deliverables may be immediately thrown away because mailing lists are over ambitious and include groups who will never use a product or support an organization. In such cases, the design may be effective, but it clearly does not deserve to exist in such a large quantity. Ensuring that design outputs target the correct audience and aren't overproduced can go a long way to increase efficiency. Similarly, designers can work with clients and stakeholders to create a robust audience profile, which can be used to evaluate whether outcomes need to be produced physically or exist in digital form instead.

Many items created by industrial designers have increased users' standard of living and made life easier and more enjoyable, but there are also a tremendous number of products that serve little purpose or duplicate the function of an existing product. Swiffer is one such example. To date, millions of people have been convinced that their brooms and mops are inadequate. Swiffer (wet and dry versions available), a device with removable parts that need to be replaced and that requires a special solution or proprietary pads, provides multitude of revenue sources for its parent company, Procter and Gamble. Clearly no one 'needs' a Swiffer. Mops (using cotton) and brooms (using straw or corn fibres) have been made of mostly natural materials in the past and are still sold, but perceived convenience and the use of persuasive advertising makes the Swiffer attractive to consumers.

3.2 Beyond Skin

Beyond Skin's designs are as stylish as they are ethically sound. Handmade in a family run company, they have a cruelty free philosophy, in terms of not only animals, but humans and the environment as well.

On-the-ground and discipline-specific realities including end-of-life issues and externalities (see page 89) need to be considered in order to ensure that success is defined by ethical and environmental goals as well as by monetary gain. Fortunately, entrepreneurs in a range of sectors are working to create consumer products that minimize the harmful environmental and social effects of production.

Beyond Skin

Natalie Dean created the UK-based brand Beyond Skin because she found it nearly impossible to find high-fashion, cruelty-free footwear. The company uses eco-friendly and recycled fabrics to produce a variety of styles of women's shoes. A clever tagline, 'genuinely not leather' is a word play on the marketing for leather shoes used by traditional footwear companies. Beyond Skin's products appeal to people who are concerned about animal cruelty and the environmental ramifications of footwear production but still want to wear fashionable shoes.

3.3

3.3 People Tree

People Tree is a pioneer in fair trade and environmentally sustainable fashion. The business was founded by Safia and James Minney to provide customers with desirable fashion, whilst working to improve the lives and environment of the artisans and farmers in developing countries who work to make the products.

People Tree

People Tree is a human-centred purveyor of clothing and homewear. The company, based in the UK, focuses on improving the lives and environment of the artisans and farmers who produce its products, while also providing customers with high-quality clothing and consumer goods. People Tree fills a special niche by partnering with Fair Trade producers in developing countries to promote economic independence for workers. The success of companies like People Tree and Beyond Skin highlights how ethically driven brands can find a loyal customer based while serving a specific cause.

People Tree's mission

- To support producer partners' efforts towards economic independence and control over their environment and to challenge the power structures that undermine their rights to a livelihood.

- To protect the environment and use natural resources sustainably throughout our trading and to promote environmentally responsible lifestyles and initiatives to create new models to promote sustainability.

- To supply customers with good quality products, with friendly and efficient service and build awareness to empower consumers and producers.

- To participate in fair trade and environmentally sustainable solutions.

- To provide a supportive environment for all stakeholders and to promote dialogue and understanding between them.

- To set an example to business and the government of a fair trade model of business based on partnership, people-centred values and sustainability.

3.4 Flow kitchen
Netherlands based Studio Gorm's sustainable 'flow kitchen' targets waste, water and energy. Kitchen scraps, newspaper and paper scraps can be composted with the built in vermicomposter and the hanging dish rack drips water directly onto the edible plants grown below. The evaporative cooling fridge box keeps food cool through evapotranspiration and is ideal for storing vegetables, fruit, eggs, cheese and butter.

3.4

How can values-driven work fit into a design practice or company?

- **Exclusive:** Ethically or environmentally based work can be the sole purview of a designer or company. In these instances the designer or studio will usually be identified as a 'green' or 'sustainable' business.

- **Partial:** A design studio or company may engage in socially or environmentally conscious work as part of their overall client base without necessarily being identified as such. In these cases, a mission or vision statement may outline the firm's commitment to the environment and to social causes.

- **Side projects or pro bono work:** Not all designers work in situations where they are able to produce environmentally or ethically based projects as part of their job. In these situations, designers may choose to partner with non-profits or community organizations and take on side projects where their work is used for the greater good.

- **Personal self-authored works:** Personal or self-authored work offers designers the opportunity to explore the themes and realities of socially and environmentally conscious design without the interference of cost issues or client stipulations. This type of work can be used as a testing ground for new ideas and unusual methodologies.

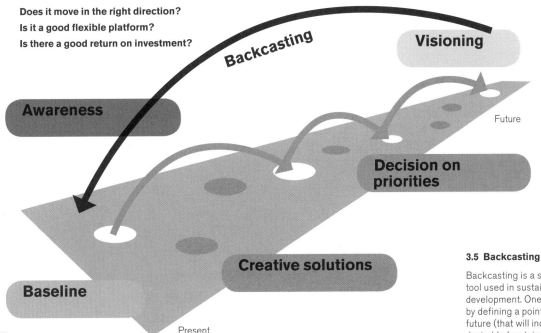

Does it move in the right direction?
Is it a good flexible platform?
Is there a good return on investment?

Backcasting

Visioning

Awareness

Future

Decision on priorities

Creative solutions

Baseline

Present

3.5

3.5 Backcasting

Backcasting is a strategic tool used in sustainable development. One starts by defining a point in the future (that will include more desirable/sustainable living standards) or by envisioning a desirable prospect and then works backwards to identify the programmes, policies and changes that will need to happen in order to connect the present to the future.

Looking into the future

Some companies and designers have begun to explore how to make design that fulfils consumer needs at the same time as they look for ways to produce more sustainable products. INAX Corporation, a Japanese manufacturer of tiling, building materials and sanitary fixtures, uses the technique of backcasting to imagine future products that have a subtly different relationship to their owners. A bath that fills with warm foam bubbles gives comfort without wasting precious water, and the company's concept kitchen provides the usual surfaces and fixtures along with built-in waste disposal, recycling systems and an innovative area for growing fresh produce.

How sustainable and ethical values fit into professional practice or a company's mandate will vary depending on the specific specialization of an individual or organization and the local context in which products are produced and sold. As explained elsewhere in this text, one designer may make environmentally preferable outputs the focus of their practice, whereas a studio or consultancy might have an underlying vision that includes ethical practice while maintaining a wide range of client services. Finally, for those who work in jobs without any values or sustainable components, there are opportunities to make real contributions by joining networks, taking on side projects and engaging in pro bono work.

3.6

3.6 Keep America Beautiful Campaign

On Earth Day 1971, Keep America Beautiful launched a campaign featuring the image of a Native American (depicted by an Italian actor) crying. Using the tagline 'People Start Pollution. People can stop it,' the campaign sought to draw attention to litter prevention, recycling and waste reduction.

Communicating values

In 1971, a public service announcement (PSA) featuring a Native American surrounded by trash began to air on TV stations across the US. Chief Iron Eyes Cody, who was played by an Italian-American actor, was crying. The spot was part of the second iteration of a campaign developed by the American Advertising Council on behalf of the environmental organization, Keep America Beautiful. With the tagline 'People start pollution, people can stop it', the message was twofold but simple. America was being damaged and defaced by pollution and citizens were encouraged to take responsibility and help keep American clean.

The Ad Council's PSA focused specifically on reducing littering by targeting a segment of the population. The Ad Council reported that in the months after the spot aired, they received up to 2,000 letters a month from people who wanted to take part in local efforts. Even more impressive, over the duration of the campaign, local groups reduced litter by as much as 88 per cent in 300 communities in 38 states. In combination with events such as Earth Day 1970, and the popularity of the high-profile book *Silent Spring* (Haughton Mifflin, 1962), the Keep America Beautiful campaign was part of a cultural shift that caused people in the US to align themselves with environmental values and to modify their behaviour because of concern for the planet.

Successful messaging

In their book *It's Not Just PR: Public Relations in Society* (Wiley-Blackwell, 2006), authors W. Timothy Coombs and Sherry J. Holladay suggest that the success of the 'Crying Indian' in the Keep America Beautiful campaign was due in large part to the threat that the advertisement implied and to the fact that the message was simple and included easy solutions. 'The threat was relevant and significant. Moreover, the response efficiency was high. It is easy not to litter and not littering will help to reduce pollution', Coombs and Holladay say. While the campaign was successful overall, Coombs and Holladay point out that the message did not result in a change of behaviour for the entire population. They think some people might not have believed the seriousness of the threat, while others might not have accepted their own responsibility or believed that the solution was actually attainable. Some viewers may even have adopted a defensive response.

According to Coombs and Holladay, no PSA can reach an entire population, but the Keep America Beautiful campaign's early use of media and marketing helped to evolve and change attitudes toward pollution and the public's responsibility toward the environment.

3.7

3.7 Keep Britain Tidy

Keep Britain Tidy launched the 'The Big Tidy Up' campaign to empower local organizations and individuals to clean up their local communities. Participants are sent a Tidy Up Kit and are given recognition awards once the tidy up has been completed. The campaign's website also includes resources and opportunities for community involvement.

Keep Britain Tidy

Keep Britain Tidy is a UK initiative. Early interventions were focused on nature destinations, such as the Lake District in England, and included anti-litter weeks and clean-up events. Later, community-based activities were augmented by successful propaganda campaigns that included anti-litter print ads and PSAs.

Keep Britain Tidy and Keep America Beautiful face similar challenges, but the tone adopted by some of the British organization's television spots and poster campaigns is edgier than those produced by Keep America Beautiful. In one memorable spot designed to target 18–24 year olds, a dominatrix puts a litterer in a latex suit and forces him to pick up garbage. Another 2002 Keep Britain Tidy poster series used images of dog excrement and tough language to encourage dog owners to be more responsible about cleaning up after their pets.

The difficulty faced by activist groups using media messaging is twofold. First, people have to care about the environment and respect public spaces, and second, a campaign must motivate actual behavioural change. The latter task is by far the most challenging and it is the one that environmental groups and activists continue to grapple with.

73

3.8

3.8 Super Cool Biz

To promote Super Cool Biz 2012 models wore traditional Japanese kimonos for the summer. The Japanese government encouraged its citizens to dress in lighter clothing to reduce the need for air-conditioning and to encourage energy savings.

Energy saving campaign

Personal gain and shared experience can be powerful motivators for lasting behavioural change and sometimes these motivators come from forces beyond anyone's control. In 2005, the Japanese Ministry of the Environment started advocating Cool Biz, a summer energy saving campaign for government employees. Air-conditioner thermostats were set at 28 degrees Celsius and office workers were encouraged to dress casually or wear special moisture absorbing materials so they could continue to be productive in warmer offices. The initial campaign had limited success with many workers continuing to wear traditional business attire, and others feeling embarrassed because they were dressed more casually than their counterparts.

However, in the summer of 2012, Cool Biz took on new urgency because it was the first time in 40 years that Japan had faced rising temperatures without the power generated from nuclear plants. Following the earthquake and tsunami in March 2011, three reactors melted down at Fukushima Daiichi nuclear plant and subsequently all the country's nuclear power plants were shut down.

Several plants have since restarted, with government officials citing the danger of a possible energy crisis, while activists argue that recent events should provide more than enough evidence that alternative means of producing energy are needed.

Keeping cool

In 2012, the government launched Super Cool Biz, a campaign that included fashion designed to mimic traditional Japanese style, but is lighter and cooler for high summer temperatures.

It is too soon to say whether the shared experience of the Fukushima Daiichi tragedy will make this iteration of Cool Biz more successful than it has been in the past, but there is widespread acceptance that campaigns are an effective means of delivering messages and promoting behavioural change. Print and television campaigns are particularly rewarding when they are paired with government incentives or community involvement, and they are often the first method applied when an organization wants to reach an apathetic and sometimes resistant population.

3.9

PLEASE REMOVE AND RETURN TO: BP INTERNATIONAL HEADQUARTERS
1 ST JAMES'S SQUARE
LONDON, SW1Y 4PD
UK

3.9 Poster competition

California-based graphic designer and illustrator Brian Hurst created this poster for the TEDxOilSpill poster competition. Most of the posters did a good job of communicating an issue or problem but this one provided viewers with a way to send BP a message. It works because it is both informative and a call to action.

Messages that work

Unfortunately, few of the problems that we face today have either simple causes or easy solutions. In many cases, this has led well-meaning environmental organizations to use species that evoke sympathy, such as whales and polar bears, as stand-ins for much more complicated systems of cause and effect. The ramifications of melting polar ice caps are far more complicated than images of a stranded polar bear would seem to suggest. The advertising industry still tends to rely on fear as a motivator when trying to garner support for environmental causes. In that respect, little has changed in the last 40 years. The problem with multi-layered issues that lack quick or clear solutions is something that plagues all sides of the sustainability movement.

3.10

3.11

3.10 Afi Mountain Reserve, Nigeria

The main town closest to Afi Mountain Reserve; smaller towns are located farther up in the hills and are accessible only by foot.

Challenges in the developing world

In the West we tend to think that we have a more enlightened view of the perils of climate change and the long-term dangers associated with the destruction of natural habitats than citizens living in developing countries do. The assumption tends to be that poorer, less-educated people are too consumed with their need to survive to care as much about the environment. Here we examine situations in Nigeria and Mozambique.

Afi Mountain Reserve, Nigeria

The difficulties faced by one set of villages in Nigeria challenge the misconception that poor people in the Third World do not care about their environment. Located at Afi Mountain near the Cameroonian border, these villages illustrate how complicated it can be to bring sustainable living conditions to developing countries where poverty, disease and hunger are the most pressing concerns. The struggle to safeguard endangered animals and rainforests, while also providing adequate resources for a local population, provides an excellent context and reality check for Western designers who may think that solving problems in the developing world is easy and can be done from a distance.

The survival of species and natural habitats is almost always inexorably linked to the livelihood and well-being of local populations. The villages located around Afi Mountain in Cross River State, Nigeria are rural. Some smaller ones are only accessible on foot or by motorbike. The land is lush, tropical and beautiful, but it is also delicate and stressed by the needs of its human inhabitants. Westerners often think the problems encountered by people living in the Third World are the result of conflicting or improper values, but the truth is infinitely more complicated.

At Afi Mountain, non-governmental organizations (NGOs) have made a substantial difference in how people regard the natural environment where they live. These villages provide a good example of the on-the-ground challenges and successes of outside intervention and aid.

NGOs making a difference

People halfway around the world cared for the animals at Afi Mountain and have donated to the Pandrillus Foundation, which means that villages have reaped benefits of increased tourism, a new market for locally grown produce, and education and training about their environment. The community-based partnerships and education of local populations have resulted in a substantial decrease in hunting. However, encroachment by small farms and loss of habitat due to burning still threatens the environment and the long-term ability of wild primates to survive in this area. Today, agriculture related activities are the greatest threat to the fragile balance that Pandrillus has worked to achieve.

Though they cover less than six per cent of the world's surface, more than 50 per cent of the plant and animal species in the world are found in rainforests. To those of us living in air-conditioned houses with plenty of food and an excess of possessions, the math is simple: we should save and protect what remains of this precious resource. Interestingly, it is unlikely that citizens living in these areas would disagree with the basic concepts of conservation and preservation. However, the reality of survival often appears at odds with the goals of preservation.

At farms near Afi Mountain, crops are grown in haphazard areas cut out of densely forested jungle. People grow food to eat and a few cash crops to sell. Those who work farms tend cocoyams (taro) and cocoa trees. Both cocoa and the bush mango seeds are too valuable for local populations to consume themselves and are sold as a cash crop instead. Similarly, most of the bananas grown in the warm and wet mountainous areas near Afi Mountain are harvested and shipped long distances and sold in cities. When people already live on so little, it is impossible to imagine how government or outside influences (even those interested in looking after the good of the planet) could forbid people to cut down rainforests and use the few resources that are at their disposal. Such regulation is simply unrealistic if it doesn't provide alternative means for local populations to survive and to better their situations.

3.11–3.13 Mezimbite Forest Centre in Mozambique

Mezimbite products are produced by hand with locally and sustainably harvested materials.

Cash crops

Agricultural cash crops are grown for sale or profit. In the developing world, cash crops are usually exported. Since prices for most cash crops are set on the international commodity exchanges, farmers may suffer because of inconsistencies in the market. Additionally, crops like cocoa and coffee have to be processed before they are used. Therefore, farmers have little use for the crop if prices fall or there is a disruption in distribution (such as may occur in times of conflict or natural disaster).

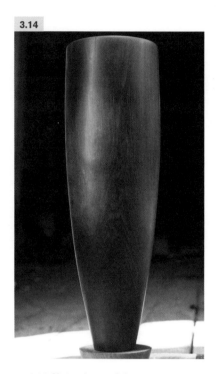

3.14 Natural materials

Schwarz's designs showcase the beauty of the natural materials found locally in the tropical and sub-tropical forests of Mozambique.

Education

It has been said that education arms people with the ability to make better choices, and while this may be true in the broadest sense, the theory presupposes that opportunities exist for an educated population. In many developing countries this is something that cannot be taken for granted. In Nigeria, Africa's most populous country, cities are full of high school and college graduates who have no choice but to open small businesses, to work odd jobs or remain unemployed because employment in their field does not exist. Lack of employment and access to education mean that in many developing countries, impoverished farmers comprise a large part of the population; and they are eking out a living in some of the world's most sensitive geographic areas. Partnering with and finding sustainable solutions for such populations should be the first line of defence against environmental destruction.

Mozambique

The Mezimbite Forest Centre in Mozambique is a community-based organization dedicated to sustainable development and design. Founder Alan Schwarz started the programme in the 1990s because he wanted to put ideas he developed as a Teaching Fellow at the Centre for Advanced Visual Studies, MIT into practice in the developing world.

All forest products (both timber and non-timber) are used to support conservation through the use of architecture, art and design, carbon sequestration, community development, environmental consulting, and the creation of fibre and textiles, food products, furniture, giftware, household goods, jewellery and personal care products.

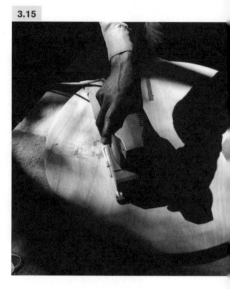

3.15 Sustainable objects

Craft workers use African noble hardwood and beeswax finishes to produce beautiful sustainable objects.

Craftspeople use hardwood to produce furniture, jewellery and housewares designed to appeal to consumers in more developed countries.

In addition to selling products and working on community-based enterprises and conservation, Mezimbite provides information about community development and conservation on its website (see www.mezimbite.com).

3.16

3.16 Maternity

Cameroonian artist and professor Idrissou Njoya has been commissioned by NGOs and other advocacy organizations to create communications pieces that use imagery to present healthcare information. As such, Njoya's work straddles the line between graphic design and fine art, but has an impact regardless of how it is labelled.

What about design?

Designers are often inclined to see real-world situations as opportunities to put their skills to use for a cause, to solve a problem, or more effectively communicate information. In reality, problems can be complicated and people may be affected both positively and negatively by changes in the environment. If one isn't careful, a can-do attitude can easily be mistaken for hubris or egotism.

Beginning in the late 1990s, Pandrillus's founders, Liza Gadsby and Peter Jenkins, spent many years along the Cameroonian and Nigerian border living and working with people in those communities. The initiatives they developed were a reaction to both the needs of local people and to the threatened species they had come to study.

Some of the case studies in this book show that the only way to be successful is to create solutions in response to real needs and to come from intimate knowledge of a situation, geographic environment and cultural milieu. In some cases, this means living where you want to affect change and in other cases it might mean working with local partners as a shortcut to the nuanced understanding of the problem. Either way, context is everything and it can be worth quieting our desire to do good until we are sure that what we propose is timely, appropriate and will actually fulfil a real need.

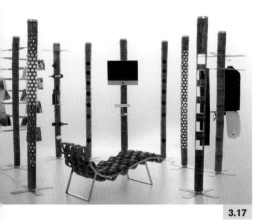

3.17

Connecting to raw materials

We tend to care more about the people and places that we have a physical or emotional connection to, so it isn't surprising there is a growing effort by designers and non-profit groups to connect consumers in the developing world with producers, environments and people in countries where raw materials are found and where goods are produced.

3.18

3.17 Bamboo

Ezri Tarazi used thick stalks of bamboo to create storage solutions for books, CDs and other media in these pieces made for the *Design for a Living World* exhibition.

3.18 FSC-certified plywood

Designers Abbott Miller and Brian Raby worked with Bolivian manufacturers to produce a chair made from sustainably harvested local wood. The chair can be shipped flat and dry assembled using a rubber mallet.

Design For a Living World

In 2009, the Smithsonian Cooper-Hewitt, National Design Museum in New York held an exhibition entitled *Design For a Living World*. The curators commissioned ten designers to develop new uses for sustainably grown and harvested materials. The designers' challenge was to tell a story about the life cycle of the materials and the role design could play to connect information about materials and their origin with consumers and viewers.

Each designer was paired with a geographical place and the exhibit featured work by Maya Lin (Maine), Isaac Mizrahi (Alaska), as well as Abbott Miller (Bolivia) and Ezri Tarazi (China). Housed in a museum rather than a store or retail environment, the resulting installations and products spanned the gamut from art to utility.

The objects were displayed in the museum within a context where viewers could understand the larger meaning. In addition to the finished artefacts, curators Abbott Miller and Ellen Lupton presented extensive documentation on the designers and included interview footage of them working with and exploring the nature of their assigned materials. Miller and Lupton recognized that storytelling is an essential tool for those working toward sustainable solutions, and that the exhibit and viewers experiences were richer for it.

Upcycling

That storytelling is needed is certain, but what is less certain is whether consumers accustomed to impulse buying have the time or inclination to make value-based purchases. If Frito-Lay's debut of 'upcycled' school supplies, which are sold at the US retail giant Target, are an indicator, then it seems big businesses are betting consumers will want to buy products that have a clever story to tell. It's true that the reused crisp-bag pencil cases retail for a mere 99 cents, but it is likely that with this product, Frito-Lay hopes to kill several birds with one stone. Not only do the cases keep used crisp bags out of landfills, but by using a recognizable bag, they provide continual brand reinforcement for the company's many products.

It's a win-win situation if consumers associate Frito-Lay with positive environmental initiatives, while tote cases are walking advertisements for Frito-Lay products.

Design for a Living World asked designers to reimagine how raw biodegradable materials could be used to create useful products, whereas Frito-Lay's reused crisp bags give the Polyethylene terephthalate (PET) bags a second use. The solutions are different but in each case designers conceived of new ways of using existing materials while also targeting consumers with information likely to make them more interested in the product.

3.19

3.19–3.20 Salmon skin

For *Design For a Living World*, designer Isaac Mizrahi created a dress and long jacket using disks of Alaskan salmon skin leather.

3.20

Upcycled

Upcycled is a term that refers to the process of converting discarded or waste materials into new usable products (often with better environmental attributes). For instance, old moth-eaten sweaters may be cut apart so the good material can be sewn together to create scarves or new clothing.

Making responsible choices

Consumers may be more likely to make purchases when a story is associated with a product, but that presupposes that relevant information about the product is available to people who want to buy it. The amount of information that even casual Internet users have access to is enormous, but usually shoppers are not making impulsive decisions based on all those specifics.

SixthSense

To connect users to metadata that is relevant but unavailable at the moment, MIT Media Lab has developed a wearable gestural interface that can sort and display pertinent information about a product. SixthSense is a wearable prototype that is made up of a pocket projector, a mirror and a camera. One of its many functions allows people to optimize decisions without requiring the users to change their behaviour. Users interact with a projection that recognizes specific gestures. SixthSense scans a barcode or uses image recognition to identify a product, then it communicates with the user's mobile phone to show data that is already available online. The projector displays a green or orange light depending on whether the product matches the user's personalized criteria.

SixthSense may not be ready for the consumer market yet, but its developers at MIT say that if the technology is mass-produced its cost would be similar to that of the average mobile phone. Systems like SixthSense offer the opportunity to help users make decisions in the moment, when it counts most, and helps to harness the overabundance of data that exists in a way that is truly useful.

3.21

3.21 SixthSense wearable computer
Pranav Mistry, electronic engineer at the Massachusetts Institute of Technology (MIT), US, operates his invention, the SixthSense wearable computer. This system allows the wearer to project digital information onto any surface and navigate the screen using hand gestures. It consists of a webcam and LED projector that hangs as a pendant from the neck and a smartphone worn on the hip.

3.22

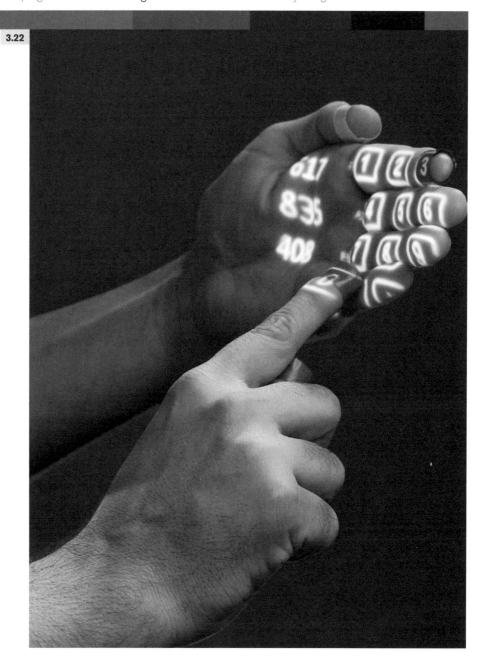

3.22 SixthSense number pad

A number pad is projected onto the palm of a hand from the SixthSense computer. This allows the wearer to project digital information onto any surface and navigate the screen using hand gestures. Colour coded tags on the fingers allow the webcam to track hand and finger movements. It then sends wireless signals to the smartphone, which contains the SixthSense software, and translates the hand gestures into computer commands.

3.23

Case study
Magno

Who Designer and social entrepreneur

What Green crafts and local jobs

Where Kandangan, Indonesia

Why it matters

Singgih S. Kartono provides employment in his local village while designing with a material that is close to his heart.

3.23 Locally sourced materials

Working with local materials allows a designer to oversee everything from the sourcing to the finished product. In this case, Kartono gives seedlings to villagers free of charge and actively promotes the replanting of harvested areas.

| Efficiency |
| Fair Trade |
| Materials |
| New markets |
| Problem solving |
| Production |
| Storytelling |

Social entrepreneurs

Numerous social entrepreneurs recognize a problem or challenge, and use entrepreneurship principles or other innovative solutions to create and manage a business or other undertaking with the goal of making positive social change.

Personal experience as motivator

Sophisticated, beautiful and meaningful are the words that Indonesian designer and social entrepreneur Singgih S. Kartono uses to describe wood, his passion and medium of choice (see www.magno-design. com). He touts its environmental benefits as well, saying that it is completely eco-friendly as long as forests are not over logged and new trees are planted to replace those that are cut down. Kartono's company, Magno, produces wooden radios that are so lovely they could be sold as sculptures. His office accessories are smaller, but equally elegant. Letter openers fit beautifully in the hand and staplers could be a centrepiece for a well-appointed desk rather than just an item of utility.

Magno trains and employs local people from the village of Kandanga where the company contributes to the local economy and helps to repair environmental damage caused by years of over logging in the area. Kartono has been able to turn wood into a profitable item that also has long-term benefits for his community.

> ' *My main idea is to reinterpret the relationship between users and the products they use. It should not be a subject-object relationship; a product is part of our life and is a "life being" too.'*
> Singgih S. Kartono, designer

3.24

3.24 Integrating technology

Since many consumers store and listen to music on MP3 players, Kartono includes a port to plug in an external device. This gives the radio additional versatility and makes it appealing to a wider audience.

3.25

3.25 Style variation

Using the same raw materials, Kartono designs various styles of radio that can be sold at different price points.

Connecting with products

In stark contrast to most appliance and technology companies, Kartono does not believe products should be built with obsolescence in mind. Instead, he strives to make objects that require no maintenance and can do everything they were intended to. The radios and other wooden products made by Magno are unfinished, one of a kind (because the texture of wood varies), and made with an absolute minimum of features. He suggests that if we are required to care for the products we own, we will be more likely to keep them. 'The built-in fragility of our products is aimed to encourage the user to be deeply connected with his or her product,' Kartono says.

Environmental crusader

When discussing design, Kartono cannot separate his role as creator from that of social and environmental crusader. Helping the people of his village, safeguarding natural resources, and making products are intrinsically linked. Kartono suggests design should be about more than just making products that are popular enough to be mass-produced. Instead, he says, 'Design must be a way to solve and minimize problems'. It might seem impossible to imagine how we could shift to making products that are more in balance with the natural world, but Kartono's design process seeks to do just that.

Kartono resists any attempts to be cast as a hero. Instead, he presents himself as a somewhat naïve businessman, though not as an accidental activist. He says he always had an understanding of local materials and a strong urge to make a positive contribution to his village.

Kandangan is located in central Java, Indonesia in an area where timber is the primary natural resource. The choice of Kandangan as the site for a design and manufacturing facility for high-end consumer goods would not have made sense to anyone from the outside. But Magno and Kartono have succeeded against the odds and have provided an excellent example of how economic and social development can go hand in hand.

Strategy in context

In Kandangan, people who have what is commonly known as 'village-grown' talent often move to the city for more opportunities and a better life. Rural areas all over the developing world include people who have received a university-level education. However, students seldom study subjects that are applicable to the places where they were born. They are often unable to make a living in their village even if they choose to return. Many are forced to look for work in cities and/or abroad in wealthier industrialized countries. This is an accelerated form of brain drain on rural communities all over the world.

In total, villages are home to the majority of the population in Indonesia (as opposed to countries where the population is greater in urban areas) and Kartono believes the role villages can play in economic development should be given higher priority. 'If thousands of small Indonesian villages could expand their socio-economic impact, together they could become a solid foundation for economic growth in Indonesia.' He suggests that if many villages could combine their resources and political voice, the result would be greater than the sum of their parts. In the meantime, villages are often forgotten by both governments and outsiders alike.

3.26

3.26 Minimal decoration
Kartono avoids decorating the products he designs. Instead he relies on the colour variation created by pairing different coloured wood with an elegant form to appeal to consumers.

3.27

3.27 Small products
Small products extend the life of wood that would otherwise be used for charcoal or to make pallets.

Using low-cost resources

Placed in the context of current concerns about climate change, Kartono feels that the deterioration of the natural environment should be a trigger that inspires us to redefine the relationship between human life and the planet and the roles we play within it. Living in a place that is already environmentally stressed, Kartono is ideally situated to see people's impact on natural systems. Forests and the wood they produce are a primary resource in Indonesia, and Kartono sees the widespread misuse of it first hand in his own village. High-quality wood is often sold as firewood and to milling factories that mostly produce shipping pallets for one-time use. These mills can use in excess of 228 trees per month. The unrelenting appetite for pallets means that forests have been depleted and younger trees are now considered to be acceptable material for pallet-making. Kartono predicts that even in areas densely forested today, there will be a shortage of usable wood if resource depletion continues at its current pace.

Do more with less

To do his part to lessen the amount of wood used, Kartono designs products and production systems that use lower-quality wood to create products that command high export prices. His goal is to use the resources that are readily available in the most efficient way. For instance, Magno is able to produce wooden radios that sell for approximately £161 (USD258) from wood that would otherwise sell for less than a dollar and would probably be burned for firewood or used to make charcoal.

Making good use of the adage, 'do more with less,' is something that Kartono strives for. 'It is possible for a small-sized product to go through a production process that consumes less material, but still requires plenty of manpower, thus creating more job opportunities to produce greater numbers of product,' Kartono says.

3.28 Employing local people

Since there is little history of local handy crafts, Kartono must train all his employees to work with the material and use the machines necessary to produce Magno's product.

Piranti Works

Magno's products are produced by Piranti Works, which is owned and operated by Kartono. This company currently employs and has trained 12 local people. Kartono plans to expand his workforce and build new workshops that will allow him to employ 40 to 50 additional employees. His system has shown that if the craftsmanship is good, then a product can sell for a reasonable price and achieve market stability.

Designer as entrepreneur

In order to grow his business, Kartono has to take on the role of manager, innovator and trainer. His workers have to be taught not only to use the equipment, but also proper workplace etiquette and to fulfil the expectations that come with regular employment. Like many entrepreneurs, Kartono wears a different hat depending on the situation and takes on duties that would belong to multiple employees in a larger company.

Working to improve both his design work and the system of manufacture allows Kartono to fulfil his goal of creating positive socio-economic impact from well-styled products. He has started a

nursery for small trees on the Magno grounds. He gives the seedlings to villagers free of charge, and he is exploring how other exotic and readily available wood, such as coffee bush and cinnamon tree, which are currently only used as firewood, can be turned into raw materials for his design work.

Kartono's challenges as a designer and entrepreneur are not unfamiliar. He is consumed by the goal of designing more useful products while using fewer resources. The production of his designs and training of new workers takes time. It can be difficult to find places to sell Magno products as he is located so far from his customers. But Kartono has achieved his goal of being able to earn a living in Kandangan, and he has managed to implement a community-based craft system that allows him to work as an industrial designer while contributing to the local economy. Kartono's genius is in his ability to fearlessly tackle numerous problems with both social and economic rewards for his company and village.

3.29

3.29 Drinking water
Plastic bags of drinking water are sold on roadsides in many African countries.

When good design goes wrong

Known as leathers in Nigeria, rubber bags in Ghana and scandal bags in Jamaica, the plastic carrier bag is both a triumph and a disaster of design. It has found its way to every corner of the earth, and it comes in as many forms as there are people who consider these cheap and disposable containers almost impossible to live without.

In the West, plastic bags hold groceries and other purchases; in the developing world they provide a handy way to grab a hot lunch and are used as a cheap and easy packaging for single servings of water sold at bus stops and along roadsides. And just about everywhere, the plastic bag is used to keep food from spoiling.

They may seem ubiquitous today, but we lived without the plastic bag for most of human history. Animal skin pouches, carved horns, ceramic jugs and later, glass containers, all provided adequate means for holding and carrying liquids. Dry goods, woven reeds, cloth and leather were fashioned into sacks and baskets by craftsmen and used repeatedly for reasons of necessity and thrift. Later, the history of single-use containment, especially of perishables, was tied to military purposes with the British Navy pioneering the use of the tin can as a way to keep food edible.

Brief history of the plastic bag

The plastic bags that are so familiar to us today were developed in the 1950s for food storage and garbage collection and by the mid-seventies large chain retailers were using them to package consumers' purchases. Interestingly, the time lag between near universal adoption of the plastic bag as a carrying device and its ban by countries overwhelmed by the waste it created is surprisingly short. It wasn't until the 1980s that the plastic bag gained full penetration in the global marketplace. Two decades later, in 2002, Ireland became the first country to introduce a tax on plastic bags. Shortly thereafter, other countries began to institute outright bans on their use.

Today, the list of countries that have heavily taxed or totally banned the plastic bag is a surprising mix of rich and poor, and bans and taxes are not concentrated in one geographic area. Consumers are charged for using plastic shopping bags in Germany and in many shops in the UK; they are taxed in Ireland and are banned outright in Rwanda, Bangladesh, and China, despite the fact that China exports millions of plastic bags to other parts of the world.

Externalities

As a design problem, the issue with plastic bags is less whether they perform their intended use and more about what happens after that use is over. It's a nasty little problem known as 'externalities'.

An externality is an unintended consequence of an economic activity where one party, who is not involved in a transaction, is affected by the transaction, product or service. Externalities can be positive or negative; they may occur during the extraction of raw materials or production, during use or at the end of a product's life cycle.

The negative impacts of a transaction that were not originally taken into account as part of normal market behaviour are referred to as 'external costs'. Externalities may affect both the consumer and the producer and, when negative, they are an excellent example of designers' and manufacturers' failure to solve an overall design problem.

Negative externalities

In the case of plastic bags, there are negative externalities at almost every stage of production and use. They can first occur during the extraction of the natural gas or petroleum. During production, harmful chemicals are used to produce polyethylene that can negatively affect people and animals if they come into contact with air or water. However, most of the negative externalities associated with plastic bags occur at the end of their life cycle. In many industrialized countries, nearly half of all plastic bags consumed are distributed by supermarkets and almost all are used for carrying items a short distance from a retailer to the consumer's home. What to do with bags after their single use remains one of the biggest challenges faced by users and municipalities, and it represents a failure in design.

Negative externalities

3.30

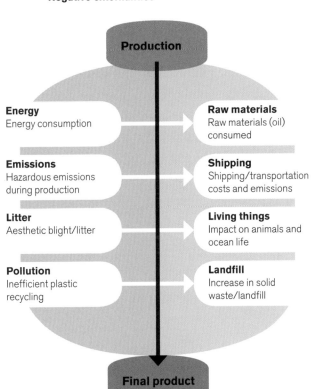

3.30 Concept of a plastic bag

The negative externalities of producing a plastic bag are illustrated in this diagram.

Energy
Energy consumption

Raw materials
Raw materials (oil) consumed

Emissions
Hazardous emissions during production

Shipping
Shipping/transportation costs and emissions

Litter
Aesthetic blight/litter

Living things
Impact on animals and ocean life

Pollution
Inefficient plastic recycling

Landfill
Increase in solid waste/landfill

3.31

3.32

The disposal problem

The lack of attention to the impact caused by a product's life cycle occurs most often when one does not have to pay for or take responsibility for the negative external costs of a product or service. The practice of ignoring objects after their usefulness has ended is not a new one. And while it is true that in previous centuries most people had little choice other than to use an object as long as was absolutely possible, once an item was discarded users had little cause to consider what happened to it.

Susan Strasser explores our complicated relationship with waste in *Waste and Want: A Social History of Trash* (Henry Holt and Company, 2000). Strasser suggests that for most of history it was only the wealthy that could afford to be wasteful. She reminds readers that before the twentieth century most Americans produced very little trash, and in the nineteenth century, trash operated in a sort of no man's land. 'Disposal (of waste) takes place in the intersection between the private and public, the borderland where the household meets the city, the threshold between male and female spheres.' If our relationship with an excess of waste is relatively new, then it is not surprising that our conception of what to do with trash is still evolving.

As Strasser suggests, despite our more frugal history, we now face a situation where a culture that embraces disposable products needs to be replaced by one that is grounded in reuse and recycling.

3.31 Pollution

Improperly disposed of waste creates an eyesore and an environmental hazard. This image of a beach strewn with trash illustrates the problem with packaging and consumer goods produced using materials that outlast a product's useful life.

3.32 Pollution under the sea

Despite recycling programmes and public awareness campaigns litter continues to be a problem. In addition to being unsightly, excess waste often makes its way into natural systems and contaminates habitat for animals and other life forms.

3.33

3.33 Plastic carrying bags

Plastic carrying bags may create a tremendous amount of waste given the brevity of their use, but plastic bags can be a relatively low impact packaging as well. Much of the milk in Bulgaria and South America is sold in a bag with a handle.

The packaging problem

Had the myriad of problems associated with the plastic bag been taken into account initially, it is unlikely these products would have found such widespread use. This is not to say that plastic or even plastic bags are always the worst packaging material. On the contrary, if one is transporting bulk items or perishable foods across great distances, plastic may in fact be the least resource-intensive and the most efficient material available.

In *Paper or Plastic: Searching for Solutions to an Overpackaged World* (Sierra Club Books, 2005), Daniel Imhoff writes extensively about the materials and technical complexities of the packaging problem. In the end though, he defines the issue as one part of a problem within interconnected systems. 'We must begin to see our purchases and their packages as part of the larger economic and cultural system,' Imhoff says. 'One should evaluate a product's applicability and success using a whole systems approach.' In such a system everything, including context, use, efficiency, production and disposal is taken into account from the start.

Alternatives to plastic bags exist, and in some cultures where other packaging systems were once the norm, the old ways have either continued or have regained popularity in recent years. Consumers in many European countries never abandoned the centuries-old tradition of carrying one's own shopping bag or basket to do their marketing.

The Japanese tradition of giving gifts wrapped in beautifully patterned cloth still survives but represents more of a token than any real decrease in use of plastic packaging. A contradiction that is highlighted when a friend arrives with a plastic shopping bag that holds a gift beautifully wrapped in cloth.

Defining success

The plastic bag is a perfect example of a common problem. It is an object that does everything it was intended to, but has consequences within its life cycle that were not considered during its design. If the success of a design is merely determined by whether or not an object achieves its intended use, we are only solving half the problem.

What is needed is a wider definition of the design problem and the adoption of holistic problem-solving methods and multi-pronged solutions. Designers can take initiative by creating more sustainable outputs, while citizens demand that their governments act responsibly to curb energy usage and create incentives for companies and organizations that are working to produce more socially and environmentally responsible goods and services.

Transporting goods will continue to be a requirement; however, the ways in which we facilitate such activities needs to be re-examined. Rather than constantly looking to new materials and technologies to solve world problems, designers can also benefit from researching how diverse populations (including those from developing countries and cultures that may live more closely with the environment) are able to store, package and move personal and food items. Sometimes rethinking common expectations and behaviours can produce more meaningful and better results than developing a new recyclable high-tech material or even monetarily encouraging waste reduction and reuse.

Tools for growing a business and predicting success

Advertising a product's environmentally preferable attributes or the fact that it was made using fair trade practices is not enough to guarantee success; nor do these attributes necessarily predict whether a market exists for a particular product or service. Audience analysis (see page 54) and benchmarking (see page 50) can be used to facilitate a designer's understanding of the context, and focus groups can reveal valuable information about consumer preferences. As highlighted elsewhere in this text, aligning the values of a company to those of its customers can also help to ensure a product receives a warm reception from buyers. However, tools for market analysis like the Ansoff Market Matrix and Product Life Cycle (PLC) can augment the preceding methods and will provide more detailed information about how the sale of product or the success of a company are likely to be impacted by market forces.

Ansoff Market Matrix

Strategist, mathematician and business manager, Igor Ansoff, developed a matrix that graphs four strategies for growth against new and existing markets (customers) and products. Ansoff's growth strategies can be used to inform business strategy and aid managers as they plan for the future and decide how to allocate resources.

- **Market penetration:** company focuses on selling existing products in current market segments to increase market share (or profitability).

- **Market development:** company targets existing products towards new markets/consumers.

- **Product development:** company develops or introduces new products to existing market segments/consumers.

- **Diversification:** company markets/creates new products for new markets.

3.34 Ansoff Market Matrix

The variables shown in this graph depict the various market factors that influence the success of a product.

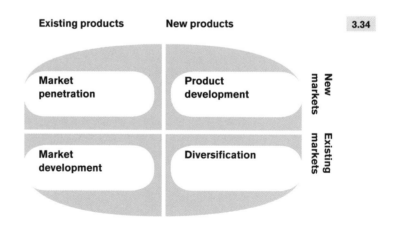

	Existing products	New products		3.34
	Market penetration	Product development	New markets	
	Market development	Diversification	Existing markets	

3.35

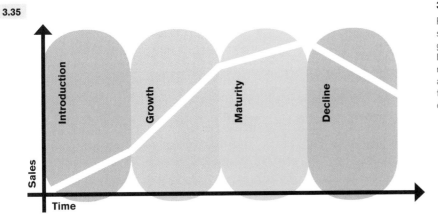

3.35 The product life cycle

Products go through a series of life cycle stages depending on market forces. This graph shows a typical life cycle of a product. It is important to note that some products may stay in one stage for longer than others and there may be products that do not seem to conform to all the stages shown on the graph.

Diversification

Diversification (strategy), as shown on the bottom right-hand corner of the Ansoff Market Matrix, has obvious applicability to the work of many designers and innovative creative studios. Diversification focuses on increasing profits through the creation of new products targeted at new markets and may require a company to obtain new facilities (or production systems), use new technologies and skills and/or partner with other firms. Diversification generally seeks to promote innovation and the theory has applicability to the work of companies such as Maruishi Ceramics Materials Co. Ltd, (see page 146) and their development of new materials, as well as for companies that may want to add a new product or service to appeal to existing or new groups of consumers.

The Product Life Cycle (PLC)

The Product Life Cycle (PLC) suggests that products go through stages from introduction, to growth, maturity and decline. These changes are associated with the market situation and will affect the revenue and profits produced throughout the life of a product. PLC theory presupposes that products have limited lives and that they pass through distinct phases, characterized by challenges and opportunities. Each stage in the life cycle may require different marketing, production, financing and purchasing strategies.

The PLC can be useful to managers and marketers as they think about positioning a product in current market situations and envision future scenarios. However, the theory has limitations. It is often difficult to identify what phase a product is in. Some products experience growth at different rates and will spend an unpredictable length of time in each phase, while other products and categories seem to be immune to decline. For design managers and strategists, the benefit of PLC may primarily be the model's focus on shifting market conditions rather than its use in forecasting future sales or the specifics of where a product is currently placed on the graph.

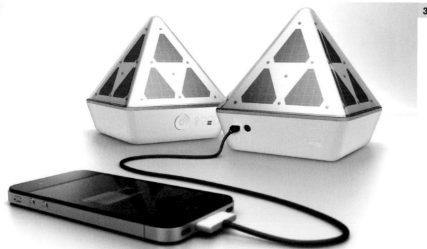

3.36

3.36 Solar light

Solar light, designed by
Disruptive Innovation (Leeds,
UK), use LCA as part of their
process and have great concept
renderings of the light and its
eco-friendly packaging.

Life Cycle Assessment (LCA)

Values-driven designers are concerned
about more than the profitability of a
company or the success of a product,
and as suggested elsewhere in this
chapter, it is important to consider all
the ramifications associated with the
production, use and disposal of
a product.

Life Cycle Assessment (also known
as Life Cycle Analysis, cradle-to-grave
analysis and eco-analysis) is a technique
for holistically assessing the impact of
a product or service from its creation
through its use and end-of-life issues.
Energy usage, raw material extraction,
materials processing, manufacture,
distribution, use, repair and maintenance,
and disposal or recycling will all be
assessed and analysed. LCAs are used
to help designers, materials engineers
and managers understand all the steps
in the life cycle of a product, to improve
processes, and to make informed
decisions. Currently, LCAs are primarily
concerned with assessing a product's
effect on the environment. Social impact
should be assessed separately, but may
complement an LCA.

3.37

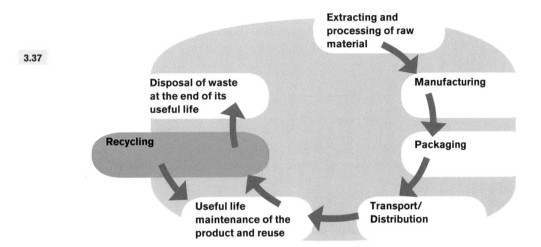

3.37 Life cycle assessment

The various stages a product goes through during its life cycle. Each of these can be evaluated for a complete life cycle assessment.

Tools and resources

Life cycle assessment often requires the input and analysis of highly technical data and conducting a full assessment may be beyond the abilities or scope of smaller design firms or individual designers. Fortunately, there are a number of online tools that make assessment easier and these resources may even include built-in data for certain materials or processes. Communications designers can take advantage of online environmental calculators provided by paper companies (most large paper companies include an environmental calculator or downloadable widget on their websites). However, for product designers and materials engineers, the process can be more complicated.

EIO-LCA

The Economic Input-Output Life Cycle Assessment (EIO-LCA) is an online tool made available by the Green Design Institute at Carnegie Mellon University (US) (commercial applications are available for license).

EIO-LCA was originally developed by economist Wassily Leontief in the 1970s. Leontief's ideas have been operationalized and updated by the Green Design Institute. The tool provides guidance on the relative impacts of different types of products, materials, services or industries with respect to resource use and emissions throughout the supply chain.

EIO-LCA and other online LCA tools are a good option for low-budget projects or in situations where the design team includes professionals with some technical expertise.

The complexity required by some assessments has given rise to a new sector of consultants, and this is a good option for larger projects or in situations where a client can afford to pay for outside services. Hiring a firm with expertise in life cycle analysis can alleviate the need for designers or strategists to get bogged down in complicated data. A consultant may have their own system for conducting an assessment, or they may use methodologies such as those developed by the International Organization for Standardization (ISO).

3.38

3.38 Eco furniture

Based in Dorset, England, Roy Tam creates small batched-produced furniture from sustainable locally sourced ash thinnings (see www.eco-furniture.co.uk).

National standards

The International Organization for Standardization (ISO) is a non-governmental organization made up of a network of the national standards institutes of 164 countries, which all participate in the development of international market-driven standards for industry. ISO acts as a bridge between public and private sectors and as such, the organization is able to develop solutions that meet both the requirements of business and the broader needs of society. ISO develops standards for good management practice and leadership, as well as for social responsibility and environmental management.

ISO 9000 and 14000 standards

ISO 9000 and 14000 are quality and environmental management standards that a company may choose to adopt; they have specific applicability to enhancing the environmental performance of an organization. A company's performance is evaluated against ISO's conformity assessment. ISO 9000 standards require the organization to commit to enhancing their customer satisfaction by meeting customer and applicable regulatory requirements.

ISO 14000 is a family of certifications that requires the organization or company to minimize the harmful effects on the environment caused by its activities and continue to improve its environmental performance. In recent years, ISO 9000 and 14000 have been adapted to target the needs of specific industries. These updated standards may be easier to adopt as they have more direct applicability to individual market sectors (see www.iso.org).

ISO standards

- Make the development, manufacturing and supply of products and services more efficient, safer and cleaner

- Facilitate trade between countries and make it fairer

- Provide governments with a technical base for health, safety and environmental legislation, and conformity assessment

- Share technological advances and good management practice

- Disseminate innovation

- Safeguard consumers, and users in general, of products and services

- Make life simpler by providing solutions to common problems

Activity: Product designers: child's toy

Children typically move from one developmental phase to another fairly quickly. This can mean that a treasured plaything or toy may become uninteresting or no longer usable in a matter of months. For this project, you will design a new toy, or redesign an existing one, to address one or more life cycle issues. The toy should be targeted at 5–8 year olds, be fun to play with, and ideally, it will have some educational benefit.

Address one or more of the following life cycle issues in toy design:

01	**Sourcing of raw materials:** Consider using low impact, natural (e.g. wood, felted wool) and/or recycled or discarded materials.
02	**Manufacture/production:** Can the toy be made by the user (DIY)? Can it be produced in a way that has minimal or no impact on the environment? Can the toy be made using cottage industry techniques or provide individuals with the means to improve their economic situation?
03	**Longevity:** Can the design encourage longer use? Can it be reused? Can components be added or subtracted? Can the toy be used in more than one way?
04	**Disposal:** Your plan may include a trade-in program and/or system for giving the toy to another child and/or if it is made of natural materials, the toy may naturally return to the environment.

Case study
Metalli Lindberg

Who Communications agency
and design laboratory

What Packaging design

Where Treviso, Italy

Why it matters

Working for Ecor, distributor of organic
and biodynamic food, the Italian
design company Metalli Lindberg finds
opportunities to rethink how consumers
can be connected to the food they eat
and the household products they use.

Consumption
Efficiency
Innovation
Materials
Problem solving
Production
Reuse/Recycling
Storytelling
Technology

Working for positive change

Located in the Conegliano Veneto
countryside in Treviso, Italy, Metalli
Lindberg is a communications agency
and design laboratory working for
positive change (see www.metalli-
lindberg.com). 'Our goal is to awaken
people's conscience, not to numb it;
to improve the world we live in, not
impoverish it,' says designer Derek
Stewart. 'In our opinion, that is what life
asks of each person.' The studio creates
communications output with the goal
of increasing the visibility of products
or brands while also enhancing the
relationship and trust that consumers
have with a client's products or services.

3.39 Ecor

For Ecor, Metalli Lindberg
worked on creating a
consistent brand image as
well as packaging the
company's products.

Design services focused on values

Metalli Lindberg's services include strategy,
consulting, research, art direction and
publishing. The company creates advertising,
print, identities, signage, interiors, websites,
packaging, exhibitions and event materials.
With an approach that is based both on science
and art, the company's designers see the
choice of an image, a graphic sign, or a font
type not as an end in itself, but as a means of
reaching a goal and of conveying a concept in
a straightforward and original way.

Using a model called 3D Communication,
Metalli Lindberg works towards objectives
and goals that include an understanding of
ethics, culture and the economy. The idea for
3D Communication arose from the desire to
make projects more effective and valuable
(ethically and environmentally) and to be able
to add to the brief without losing sight of the
client's needs. Balancing these factors means
more work for designers but it makes the job
more fulfilling as well. Stewart explains, 'We try
to take all these considerations into account
before going to market or before marketing
comes into the picture.' Their approach is not
unique, but having an individualized framework
does help the company make work that fulfils
its mission and makes it easier to talk to clients
about the value of including sustainability
and social consciousness in communications
design outputs.

3.40

3.40 Ecor logo

Drawings documenting the development of the Ecor logo.

Planning and strategy

Strategy and consulting allow Metalli Lindberg to supplement the traditional competencies of a creative agency. Even when a project comes with a defined brief, they try to add value and, at times, the designers may even put the brief aside and look for new ways to enhance the solution without alienating the client or ignoring the objectives for intended outcomes.

Their work often involves diagrams and outlines that illustrate how the market for a product is developing, changing or even lacking. Stewart believes consulting can help foster better relationships with clients. Being fully embedded in the planning stage also makes clients feel more comfortable with the creative process and provides greater opportunities for designers. 'When you are brought in at the development stage, you can propose new ideas and look for opportunities that aren't necessarily outlined in the brief,' he says.

Thinking beyond

Metalli Lindberg employed a multifaceted strategy-based approach when they were asked to create a print campaign for the manufacturer of office furniture. For the first phase of the project, the team came up with the heading 'design + beyond', which was used on promotional materials for a trade show and in print ads for UK magazines.

The slogan 'design + beyond' was a test for a broader initiative called 'Thinking Beyond'. This new statement highlighted the company's vision and mission, and was able to encompass all the company's activities including: design, strategy, research of materials to new processes, as well as their concern for the well-being of their employees and respect for the environment. As a visual representation of that promise, Metalli Lindberg created a mark/logo, which appeared as a sticker or label on their products, packaging, brochures, stores and on exhibition stands. The logo acted as a kind of 'guarantee', an affirmation that was embraced by both the client and consumers alike. The effectiveness of the campaign is demonstrated by the fact that more than five years later the company still uses Metalli Lindberg's ideas and designs even though they are no longer a client.

3.41

3.41 Ecor's product line

Ecor's product line is bright and colourful and uses illustration rather than photographs of food to encourage consumers to purchase their organic and biodynamic products.

3.42

3.42 Packaging

Whenever possible Metalli Lindberg
tries to use one package type for
more than one product and varies
the colour of ink and design so that
products can be shipped to stores
efficiently and use a minimum of
packaging.

Diverse outputs

For Ecor, a large distributor of
organic and biodynamic food, Metalli
Lindberg's designers imbue the
company's overall brand, packaging
and communications strategy with
ethics and relevance. Designers work
to balance costs without losing sight
of cultural context and the customer's
needs and requirements.

Ecor has a catalogue that includes
thousands of products, and with
20 years' experience, the company
is one of Italy's largest distributors
of organic and biodynamic food.
Working closely with Ecor, Metalli
Lindberg provides a range of services
including consulting, research,
strategy, placement analysis, art
direction, advertising and packaging.
Ecor's products are diverse and
Metalli Lindberg has created
packaging for its rice, pasta, muesli,
biscuits, canned beans and fruit juice.

Challenges

The issues Metalli Lindberg encountered
when trying to create eco-friendly and socially
responsible packaging for Ecor are remarkably
similar to any other design problem:

- Solutions must be simple and still
  remain effective.

- Labels should be identifiable as a family
  of products and subsequent sub-families.

- Graphic format must be chosen that
  is easy to implement as new products
  are introduced.

- All graphic solutions must support
  a strong identity/brand.

- Packaging should be informative where
  possible (stating organic farming).

- Legibility/clarity is essential in
  understanding certification, origins
  and recipes.

- Solutions should communicate the cultural
  value of organic agriculture and
  its traditions/origins through imagery.

- Physical production requires choice and
  minimal use of materials, which should
  be ecological where possible.

3.44

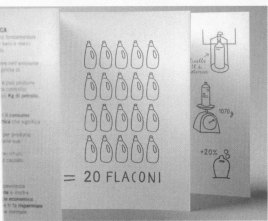

3.43

3.43 Ecoriciclo

Consumers are hungry for information about environmentally preferable products, so Metalli Lindberg's work for Ecor included informational brochures explaining the benefits of the Ecoriciclo system (see page 102).

Packaging and behavioural change

The physical form that packaging takes remains a dilemma as the process may involve a long chain of suppliers, and costs need to be considered. Metalli Lindberg's solution has been to use only one material where possible and to minimize the use of materials including paper, plastic and even inks. The company recently completed a project for a fresh vegetable tray and wrapping where the tray, plastic wrap and sticker were all compostable. Regardless of the aesthetic form that packaging takes, Metalli Lindberg's designers are always conscious of the larger challenge when dealing with food consumption. Stewart suggests that the work of designers needs to be supported by more widespread 'behaviour change'. Consumers also need to be 'more selective about what they buy, where it comes from and the amount of waste that is generated during production and packaging, and also at home with unused food being thrown away.'

Biodynamic food

Biodynamic food is produced by biodynamic agriculture, which uses the forces in nature to achieve a balance in the interrelationships of land, plants and animals so a self-nourishing system is created that does not need chemical fertilizers or other external inputs. Originating with the work of Rudolf Steiner, an Austrian-born philosopher and social thinker, biodynamic agriculture was one of the first ecological farming systems. It focuses on the observation of natural systems and uses that information to disturb the land and cycle of life as little as possible.

3.45

3.44–3.45 Ecor's home products

Selected products from Ecor's home product range.

Ecoriciclo

To radically shift the footprint of packaging, it is sometimes necessary to reconceive how products are distributed. Metalli Lindberg did just that for Ecoriciclo, Ecor's initiative to have consumers refill containers in the store.

Ecoriciclo reduces the use of plastics and drastically lowers the number of plastic bottles used by consumers, saving both the company and shoppers money. Essentially a bulk type of shopping experience, Ecoriciclo has developed specific bottles that one refills with only one product. Customers are charged a small initial fee for bottles, which are specifically designed to be refilled. Checkout is a seamless experience since each bottle has its own barcode. Ecoriciclo is promoted in shops that carry Ecor products and the self-service taps are positioned near checkout areas where assistance and explanatory materials are available.

Recycling shopping bags

When asked whether it is realistic to expect consumers to save and reuse packaging, Stewart points to the success of recycling shopping bags. He says it's a fairly common practice in Italy, but concedes that incentives are still necessary for people to adopt environmentally friendly practices. To this end, Ecor provides a selection of environmentally friendly shopping bags made with either MaterBi®, compostable paper bags made from discarded Tetra Paks, or organic cotton reusable shopping bags, which it offers to consumers at reduced prices. Additionally, initiatives like Ecoriciclo are cost effective and Ecor is able to pass on those savings to shoppers.

Good communication

Maintaining a close relationship with their client has allowed Metalli Lindberg greater freedom when designing, while offering the company the opportunity to continue to make work that strives to combine economy, aesthetics and ethics. The end result of this method for design problem solving is that 'communication is visible, tangible and represents an intelligent and positive investment'. All of these factors support Metalli Lindberg's goal of contributing to the world in which it resides, while disseminating values that include ethics, sustainability and cultural relevance.

3.46

3.47

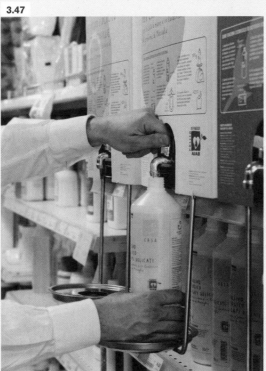

3.46–3.47 Ecoriciclo

The Ecoriciclo system allows consumers to refill containers in the store. Specially made packaging for both the refillables and the bulk detergents makes refilling a breeze and cuts down on spillage and other issues that are sometimes associated with in-store bulk buying.

Activity: Communications/advertising designers

Most consumers only interact with a product during the use and disposal phase of the product life cycle. However, people are more likely to take action or make responsible choices when they more fully understand how a product impacts the planet. For this activity, you will redesign the packaging of an existing product to communicate life cycle issues associated with the product.

01	Choose a popular consumer product and analyse which are the most pressing environmental issues associated with its life cycle (use online research, information provided by the company and free LCA tools).
02	Using brainstorming techniques, generate several ways in which environmental issues can be mitigated. You can focus on sourcing of raw materials, manufacture, distribution, use or disposal/recycling.
03	Consider how best to communicate with the intended audience and list what visual techniques can be used to provide information about the life cycle of the product.
04	Analyse whether the current packaging is wasteful or uses inefficient or environmentally harmful materials. Consider using info graphics and/or diagrams as a communicative device.
05	Create a report/plan to be given to the company that produces the product. The report should include: a Analysis of life cycle issues. b Benefits and shortcomings of existing packaging. c Proposal for package redesign.

4.1 Red forest rug

The red forest rug was designed
by Chris Haughton as part of
the NODE project. The aim was
to combine brilliant design with
good, fair trade projects in order
to make as much impact for fair
trade as possible.

CHAPTER 04

Design Making Change

Over the past decade, collaborative endeavours have gained popularity in the design community and are used by agencies and studios as a way to maximize creative potential. While partnerships are most commonly used for commercial purposes, they can also help to connect designers with community-based causes and professional opportunities that allow people to express personal values (with or without monetary compensation).

The Internet, social media sites, and online groups have made it easy to find and communicate with like-minded citizens regardless of geographic location, and designers can choose to use these resources as part of client-based practices, or as a way to forge links between their own ideas and the needs of various stakeholders and community organizations.

4.2

4.3

4.4

4.2 Plant the Peace

As part of Plant the Peace, a touring exhibition, designers Chris Humes and Noah Scalin created a 9 mm shooting pistol.

4.3–4.4 Shooting for a cause

The concept was that Instead of bullets, the guns shoot local seeds and can be used for gardening.

Technology facilitating collaboration

With greater awareness of social and environmental issues comes an increase in demand for resources that examine how design thinking/making can be used to promote meaningful and lasting community-based change. Many online cause-based organizations help to facilitate collaboration between individuals interested in pursuing values-based design. In some cases, members can choose to work on a project or topic that resonates with them personally, whereas other organizations strive to connect designers in industrialized countries with producers in countries with emerging economies. In either case, the use of technology can facilitate partnerships between users of diverse backgrounds in a way that would have been difficult a decade ago.

Opportunities for service

While it is attractive to be able to collaborate with partners remotely, some designers are motivated to make a more substitutive change in their professional practice. These individuals can also use online groups and non-profits to connect to work or volunteer opportunities. In the US, AIGA's Design for Good is an online platform that helps partner organizations and design groups create positive social change (www.aiga.org/design-for-good). Design for Good empowers designers through online networking tools, chapter events, training, national advocacy and promotion. The initiative also connects designers and partner organizations to fund-raising opportunities and resources.

In the UK, VSO (see www.vso.org.uk) places volunteers with skill-specific opportunities in emerging economies (see page 111). A placement as an embedded volunteer can have repercussions beyond the time spent in service. The experiences and skills learned volunteering or working as part of pro bono projects can act as a starting point and provide experience for designers who want to reframe their professional practice to focus primarily on social and environmental causes.

Management tools for collaboration

Employees and volunteers working on cause-related projects are often highly motivated to create first-class results and meet deadlines. However, when more than one person works on a project, some degree of management is needed. A loose collaboration may require team members to communicate via email and have periodic conversations to assess progress and decide on the overall direction. But for larger jobs and in design studios, a single person is often designated as a project manager. That person interfaces with clients or organizational partners (as is the case of some cause-related work) and may use software systems and other business-related tools to keep track of deadlines, assess progress and facilitate collaboration.

In addition to the practical considerations associated with collaboration, it may be necessary to educate stakeholders and clients about the design process and any specific techniques or ways the group goes about approaching creative problems. Once a working process has been developed, the team may generate a visual representation of the customized problem-solving process. These diagrams are particularly useful when one is working with partners who have little experience and/or understanding of the design process. They can be used to educate viewers about creative endeavours, to address business and cause-related issues, and to describe the specifics of a working process.

4.5

4.6

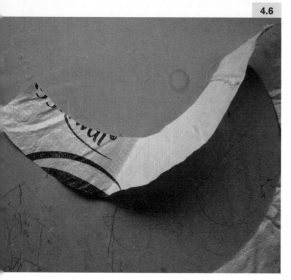

4.5–4.6 Polypropylene hat
The Element 21 hat is made with woven polypropylene (PP) plastic that is used as packaging for various foodstuffs, including rice and other staples. The polypropylene is light, impermeable to water, foldable and easily washed.

How to design for a cause (even at home)

What does it mean to design for a good cause and how can one be an agitator, an organizer and an agent of change? Good design is made by professionals who care. Whether working alone or in collaboration with like-minded organizations, designers have the tools to be catalysts and make a positive impact at home, in their communities and around the world. Design for a cause starts with doing what we do best and being flexible to a range of communication modes and outcomes.

First-year design students are often asked what it is that they will produce when they finish college. Their list can become dizzyingly long. Some designers may spend a whole career mastering the intricacies of user-interface design, while others create environmental graphics and signage for a museum one week and layout an annual report the next. Similarly, the ways designers can help to organize and generate opportunities for participation among audiences and consumers is as diverse as the output that they make.

Whether designers build better experiences for viewers or develop sites to help citizens organize and campaign for change, they have an opportunity to align themselves with causes that they believe in. The results are rewarding, stimulating and can add some excitement to the design experience.

Small steps

Thinking in terms of scale can be paralysing and even activists can get discouraged by how much there is to do. Fortunately, small steps are just as important as large initiatives. Mentoring a student from an underprivileged background or taking on an intern and helping them to do values-based work can have far-reaching effects. If every designer acted as a catalyst in some small way, the net gain would be tremendous. When we begin to think of motivating people toward action, we should start by making connections with like-minded individuals. Live by doing. It inspires others to do the same and there is lasting value in making design for good. No job is too small to start creating work that makes a positive impact.

4.7

4.8

4.7 Element 21
Geneva-based non-profit, Element 21 makes patterns for do-it-yourself products available free of charge. People make their own hats and bags for fun. The organization also works with craft groups in emerging economies where Eurocentric designs provide a revenue stream for its producers (see www.element21.ch).

4.8 Materials for the hat
Materials needed to produce the hat are simple and include discarded polypropylene and a small piece of denim or other cloth for the hat liner, scissors, a pen, ruler, thread and a sewing machine.

Five ideas to explore when making socially or environmentally responsible design:

1 Ask yourself, 'What are my strengths?' Once identified, look for opportunities based on those attributes.

2 Ask yourself whether you can do values-based work where you are employed. If so, then you might already be doing good. If not, consider whether fellow employees have ideas or beliefs in common – if so there might be opportunities to collaborate and work on ethical design projects.

3 Are there areas of your life, such as hobbies, faith, family or community, that are particularly meaningful? If so, look for ways to interface with an organization or group that is already part of your life or one that is aligned with something that interests you. Put your skills to use, whether they are in design, communication or organization.

4 Keep doing what you do best as an individual. It might seem like a cliché, but much would be accomplished if we all 'used the force' for good. This might mean designing a typeface for the visually impaired, or working in local schools so that children understand the importance of design in the world. It is about your skills, your interests and your change.

5 Avoid getting bogged down in the bigger questions, or single-handedly trying to save the world. First consider contributing locally, at work or in your community. Then if you have the energy, go ahead and tackle a global initiative.

Be a designer... for good

With the world's population predicted to exceed seven billion in 2013, it is safe to say that none of us are really alone. But for designers who are interested in working for the greater good, it can be difficult to connect with like-minded enthusiasts. Social media and networking sites provide groups for origami buffs and kite makers, so it is no surprise they are also offering ways for designers to connect with each other. You can join the green professionals group on LinkedIn, and find out about local energy-saving events through Facebook. If you are interested in even more ways to make connections, there are numerous groups bringing together designers with partners who are also interested in contributing to social and environmental causes.

Organizing and agitating for change

As mentioned in chapter 1, sites such as www.livingprinciples.org harness the Internet to connect like-minded individuals in diverse locations. Members create profiles and in a Wiki-like format and upload ideas, share projects, and exchange information. Similarly, Memefest Kolektiv (see www.memefest. org) is an international network based in Slovenia and Australia whose founders are primarily interested in promoting social change through the use of media and communication.

Media-based initiatives

Memefest hosts an annual 'Festival of Socially Responsive Communication and Art', and allows members to communicate, collaborate and share ideas via blogs and other social media formats. Learning about new ideas and market-specific improvements is just as important as finding collaborators and partner organizations. For information about how to connect social and environmental issues to business strategy, check out Big Picture TV (see www.bigpicbiz.com). This UK-based site is a good resource for information about current trends related to the environment and social initiatives. Watching featured videos is a great way to learn about the work and ideas of leading scientists, economists, environmentalists and entrepreneurs.

Design Ignites Change

Design Ignites Change (see www. designigniteschange.org) is a collaboration between Adobe Foundation and Worldstudio Foundation. The organization provides guidance on how to run social-change projects for students. Through their mentoring programme, college students and professional designers work with high-school students to create projects based on a social theme. Design Ignites Change offers resources on how to secure funding and honours innovative projects with awards. Project examples are showcased on the Design Ignites Change website.

4.9

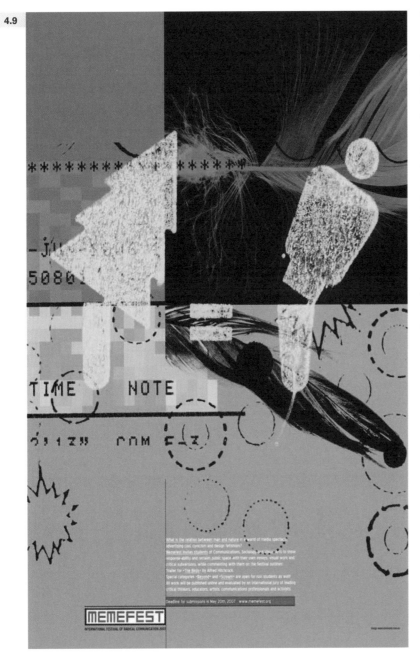

Voluntary Service Overseas

Even though making work locally can be just as important as making a contribution in another country, some designers feel the call to serve and the call to travel at the same time. Voluntary Service Overseas (VSO) is a UK-based international development organization that works with volunteers to fight poverty in developing countries. Placements are three months to two years and are based on an individual's skills, interests and the needs of communities in the countries where VSO works. The organization is not design-specific, but its focus on pairing volunteers with partners and NGOs that require a specific skill means that designers can end up working for a variety of causes in any of VSO's 40 partner countries.

4.9 Memefest poster
Memefest encourages the sharing of ideas about social change through the use of media and the connectivity of the Internet.

Working close to home

In Geneva, Switzerland, designer Guido Styger has created a network for designers interested in using problem-solving and design skills to work on local problems, while providing innovative solutions that can be applied by communities in the developing world. Element 21's projects are very diverse. They include parties to raise awareness, a plan to utilize dog waste to generate biogas and fertilizer, and ways of encouraging landlords to make buildings more energy efficient. Styger says it is important to keep context in mind and look for ways of contributing locally. He suggests that people who live in a place often have the best ideas when it comes to solving local problems. He points out that Element 21's initiative to create incentives for landlords to put in solar power and make energy-saving renovations is particular to Switzerland, where over 60 per cent of the population rents rather than owns a home.

Styger goes on to say that outsiders often have difficulty understanding the intricacies of local governments and systems. This can impede progress and can lead to solutions that do not work in a particular environment.

Much of Element 21's work is focused in Geneva, but their initiatives include making information and design expertise available online. The group provides free patterns for products that will appeal to European consumers. These can be downloaded on the Internet and used by producers in emerging economies to target a wider consumer base.

Styger believes that offering long-distance design services to those who are less fortunate is a smart use of resources and ultimately benefits both people living in emerging economies and those in industrialized countries.

Collectif Solaire

Collectif Solaire is a project to encourage tenants to collectively invest in solar collectors for heating. This creates a system for safe communal deposits, which can go towards the cost of purchasing and installing solar collectors. The benefits include a 40 per cent reduction in energy bills that will pay back the tenant's initial investment over time. In this system, tenants pay less for energy, the landlord has a more valuable building, and energy savings benefit the environment.

4.10 Solar collectors

The Swiss generally rent their homes. Home ownership is lower than in other industrialized countries and since tenants pay their own energy bills, Swiss landlords have little incentive to adopt energy-saving solutions.

4.11 The dogs of Geneva

The city of Geneva has about 35,000 registered dogs, which is high compared to other townships in Switzerland. The dogs of Geneva produce approximately 1,800 tons per year of excrement.

4.12 Caniplus project

Element 21's Caniplus project proposes that instead of burning collected dog waste, it be used to produce biogas and fertilizer, thereby reducing the environmental impact and public cost of disposal. This would turn dog waste into a resource producer.

4.13

4.13 Project H

Educational environments developed by Project H Design have been used both in the US and the developing world. The playgrounds, made with inexpensive materials, can be used to teach a variety of skill sets, while engaging energetic young school students.

4.14

4.14 Studio H

Studio H is a one-year high school programme for the Bertie County School District in rural North Carolina, which combines design thinking, vocational training, and community citizenship to equip low-opportunity teenagers with critical creative problem-solving skills for life.

Project H Design

Emily Pilloton developed Project H Design as a way for designers to collaborate and solve problems at home and around the world. Volunteer designers are dedicated to using design to make a difference. Project H participants respond to real needs identified in various communities and work with international partners and other experts to create solutions that can be applied successfully near home or in more distant settings.

Pilloton, who has achieved notoriety in the design community by being interviewed on the Colbert Report, writing *Design Revolution: 100 Products That Empower People* (Metropolis Books, 2009), and lecturing widely, moved the headquarters of Project H Design from San Francisco to rural Bertie County, North Carolina in 2010. As the poorest county in North Carolina, Bertie County provides an opportunity for Pilloton to put her credo of 'working in one's own back yard' into practice. She and her partner Matthew Miller now live in a place with opportunities to explore how design can affect change in schools, where one in three children live below the poverty line. Project H Design's initiatives include playground teaching environments and the design of computer labs.

Networks creating change

Creating change is not always about producing objects or even conveying information. Sometimes challenging people's thinking or exploring cultural norms and individuality can be just as revolutionary as a new product. INDIGO is an international indigenous design network that is sponsored by Icograda, the international design organization. The network is a participatory platform that encourages designers to explore their understanding of indigenous design and local design.

INDIGO invites designers to consider themes such as colonization, migration, politics, language, history, identity, and conditions such as the economy and natural resources. Through INDIGO's Mother Tongue initiative, designers are invited to submit posters to an online exhibition that seeks to capture the power of language – verbal and visual, formal and informal.

Networks to join

Design 21: Social Design Network
www.design21sdn.com
Design 21 seeks to inspire social activism through design. The site connects people who want to explore ways that design can positively impact our many worlds and who want to create change.

Design For Good
www.aiga.org/design-for-good
Design for Good is a platform that creates opportunities for designers to build their practice, their network and their visibility while using design thinking to advocate and work for social change.

Design Ignites Change
www.designigniteschange.org
Design Ignites Change engages high school and college students in multidisciplinary design and architecture projects that address pressing social issues.

The Designers Accord
www.designersaccord.org
The Designers Accord is a global coalition of designers, educators, and business leaders working together to create positive environmental and social impact. Adopters of The Designers Accord commit to five specific guidelines that provide collective and individual ways to take action.

Element 21
www.element21.ch
Element 21 is a network of designers committed to solving local and international problems through innovative and creative solutions.

INDIGO
www.indigodesignnetwork.org
INDIGO is an open network connecting designers around the world with the goal of understanding the notion of indigenous design.

The Living Principles
www.livingprinciples.org
The Living Principles aims to guide purposeful action, celebrating, and popularizing the efforts of those who use design thinking to create positive cultural change.

o2 Global Network
www.o2.org
o2 Global Network is an international network on sustainable design. o2 organizes workshops, lectures and informational material to promote and implement design for sustainability.

Project H Design
www.projecthdesign.org
Project H Design connects the power of design to the people who need it most and the places where it can make a real and lasting difference.

Voluntary Service Overseas
www.vso.org.uk
VSO is a UK-based independent international development organization that works with volunteers to fight poverty in developing countries.

Case study
Chris Haughton

Consumption

Fair Trade

Materials

New markets

Problem solving

Production

Storytelling

Who Designer and social entrepreneur

What Soft toys, carpets, bags and other retail products

Where UK-based designer working in Nepal

Why it matters

By working with fair trade organizations in Nepal, Chris Haughton is able to provide work opportunities for locally trained artisans, while creating products for the European retail market.

4.15

4.15 Weaving rugs

A textile worker weaving a rug for NODE.

On the ground in Nepal

UK-based illustrator and children's book author Chris Haughton arrived in Nepal in March 2010. Haughton, who had spent several years doing freelance work for People Tree, the London-based fair trade retailer, believed he could easily adapt his work to fit the criteria needed to create non-industrialized textiles and other products. He set about creating partnerships with local cooperatives that produce fair trade items to be sold in the UK and Europe.

Back in London, Haughton's experience of working in advertising and commercial design was disillusioning. Commercial work may have been financially rewarding but it often did not complement his values. In recent years, he has found that fair trade could provide a starting point to rethink the way he produced work. 'I am very grateful to the people I have met in fair trade who have reminded me again what good design can be,' he says.

4.16

4.16 A Bit Lost

For his book, *A Bit Lost* (Candlewick/ Walker, 2011), Haughton designed a soft toy to accompany the book. The owl is made by workers at Mahaguthi (see www.chrishaughton.com).

4.18

4.17 Making owls
Haughton designed the owl to be flat
so it could be packaged with his book.
The toy is made from raw cotton, which
is hand-spun into yarn, dyed, and finally
sewn by the women at Mahaguthi.

4.18 Fair trade toys
Fair trade toys made by NODE
(see www.madebynode.com).

Mahaguthi school

After four months in Nepal, Haughton
had worked on a variety of projects with
a number of fair trade organizations.
At the Mahaguthi school, Haughton
designed a soft toy to be made entirely
from scratch by the workers. It sells as
a companion to a children's book he
has written, *Little Owl Lost* (Candlewick
Press, 2010). The toy is produced using
raw cotton using traditional cottage
industry techniques that Mahatma
Gandhi (1869–1948) made famous.
For Haughton, Nepal has been an
opportunity to do something different.
'It has led my own work to evolve in lots
of new and unexpected directions,'
Haughton says. 'I would definitely
recommend similar partnerships
to other designers.'

Mahaguthi, which means 'craft with
a conscience', has a long history of
social activism. Haughton was eager to
work with them as he sees their work
as epitomizing fair trade. The school
was founded in 1923 by legendary
social reformer Tulsi Mehar Shrestha
(1896–1978). Mehar campaigned against
the inequalities of the rigid Nepalese
class structure in which only high-caste
men were educated and where there
were few or no opportunities for women.
Shrestha worked with Gandhi and the
two had a single vision to empower
women through education and income-
generating projects so they could
become self-sufficient.

With a donation from Gandhi, Mehar set
up a spinning and weaving development
project that became Mahaguthi. The
project was the first of its kind in
Nepal and was among the first-ever
manufacturing units in what was, at
the time, an economically closed and
feudal country. Mahaguthi currently
takes on 90 new women a year, most of
whom are widows or victims of domestic
abuse. The women's children are sent to
primary school, while their mothers learn
employable skills and are taught to read.

Designing textiles

For years, Haughton had converted digital
illustration files to screen prints for inclusion
in exhibitions and shows. In Nepal, he had the
opportunity to turn these same illustrations
into rugs. For this project, Haughton worked
with the Kumbeshwar Technical School,
where he found students with the expertise
to produce natural hand-spun Tibetan wool
carpets. Introduced to Kumbeshwar, through
his client People Tree, the school trains
lower-caste men and women, and supports
a primary school with 260 students and an
orphanage with 19 children. Haughton found
the carpet-making process was similar to the
pixel make-up of digital images and was able
to easily transfer his digital designs to carpet
patterns. Working with the design team at
Kumbeshwar, Haughton was able to convert
his digital images directly to carpet graphics.

Together with Akshay Sthapit, Haughton has
set up NODE, a non-profit social business
to connect designers to this fair trade
project. They have created a collection that
features 18 well-known designers who have
each been asked to design a rug. Geoff
McFetridge, Donna Wilson, Sanna Annukka
and Chamo are some of the artists involved
in the project. The rugs are available at the
Design Museum shop in London (UK).

Association for Craft Producers

ACP is a local, not-for-profit fair trade organization providing design, marketing, management, and technical services to low-income Nepalese craft producers who blend traditional craft with modern design and technology to suit market trends (see www.acp.org.np).

Kumbeshwar Technical School

KTS provides vocational training for women and young men in carpet weaving, hand knitting, and carpentry. KTS supports and funds its fair trade programmes through the sale of high-quality fair trade carpets, knitwear and furniture (see www.kumbeshwar.com).

Mahaguthi: craft with a conscience

Mahaguthi is a fair trade organization that produces, markets, and exports Nepalese crafts. It serves both the domestic and international markets and has three shops in the Kathmandu Valley (see www.mahaguthi.org).

People Tree and ACP

For his original client, People Tree, Haughton partnered with ACP to develop products for the company's retail stores and catalogue, which included soft toys, bags, rugs and cushion covers, which can also be sold domestically in Nepal. ACP is the largest fair trade group in Nepal, and the organization supports thousands of women. It offered Haughton the chance to create a range of products through a single partnership.

Haughton cites People Tree as an example of a company that is using fair trade manufacturing to make products responsibly. 'Increasing fair trade manufacturing would be a really powerful force in poverty reduction,' Haughton says. 'What's missing is design. There are some amazing traditional crafts that are perfect to produce high-end designer products'. Haughton sees textiles as an area that particularly lends itself to such partnerships and feels that textile designers would be surprised at the techniques available for creating high-quality products.

4.20

4.20 Woollen rug
At Kumbeshwar Technical School, students produce all-natural, hand-spun woollen rugs.

4.19

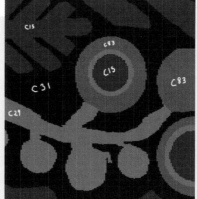

4.19 Test grid
Haughton made the first test grid digitally. Colour specification is key, and he says 'I managed to mess up and specify C31 (beige) instead of C30 (black).'

4.21

4.21 Fair trade bags
Production of fair trade certified bags that were designed by Haughton for People Tree.

118

Fair trade practices

Haughton is committed to fair trade practices and is deeply frustrated by the lack of market penetration that the fair trade manufacturing mark has achieved. Unlike the commodity mark, which is widely recognized and overseen by Fairtrade Labelling Organizations International (FLO), the manufacturing mark is relatively unknown to consumers and is regulated by the World Fair Trade Organization (WFTO). Haughton postulates that the problem may be because the items that use the fair trade raw commodity mark 'can sell themselves without much help from the designer.'

Products regulated by the WFTO require a more complicated system since they have to be designed and produced in a way that appeals to consumers while following the organization's regulations. More than 50 per cent of UK consumers now recognize at least one of the fair trade marks.

When asked about the benefits of fair trade in the overall war against global poverty, Haughton says that he cannot see any other viable way past capitalism and its inequities. 'Fair trade has so much potential because it uses the best parts of an imperfect system,' he says. Getting to make fun carpets, bags and soft toys is the stuff that designers dream about. Doing it in a way that supports fair wages in the developing world is enough to keep Haughton looking for new ways to apply his designs and illustrations to traditional craft production and low-scale manufacturing for many years to come.

Fair trade labelling

Two main certification marks govern fair trade. The first is the Fairtrade Labelling Organizations International (FLO), which oversees commodities such as coffee, tea, and fruit and is the most widely recognized (see www.fairtrade.net).

The second is the World Fair Trade Organization (WFTO), whose members oversee the more complex fair trade manufacturing certification. Clothing, stationery, handicrafts, and manufactured goods all come under this mark, so it is the place to go for designers who want to create and manufacture fair trade products. Membership in the WFTO is limited to organizations that demonstrate a 100 per cent fair trade commitment and apply its 10 Principles of Fair Trade (see www.wfto.com).

4.22

4.22 Fair trade marks
The logo for Fairtrade Labelling Organizations International (FLO) and the logo for the World Fair Trade Organization (WFTO).

4.23

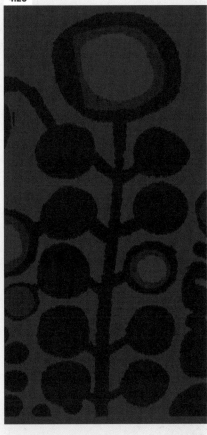

4.23 Mayan red rug
Haughton and the school's design team found a way to easily convert his illustrations into carpet graphs, a process that he hopes will make carpet-making easier.

Activity: Working with partners

Chris Haughton has found partners in the developing world to produce products they can sell to retailers in the UK. Imagine you were trying to do the same thing. What could you produce and with whom would you work?

01	Read about the organizations that Haughton has partnered with. What could you create if you were to partner with these groups?
02	Create your own carpet design. Which target market would it be designed to appeal to? What kind of pattern/design would you use and why?
03	Think about new markets for the goods you have created. Where would the products be sold? How would you ensure that workers received fair wages? How would consumers know and value the socially responsible decisions that went into making these products?

Managing effective collaboration

Concept development and design execution almost always require some degree of planning, but how a manager's role is defined varies depending on the context, size and scope of a project. A manager works to understand the project, defines outcomes, plans how objectives are to be achieved (including incremental steps), monitors process and assesses results. A good manager makes a designer's work easier, respects others, strives to maintain good working conditions, provides opportunities for growth, and makes sure that team members are fairly compensated.

Some people are naturally suited to management, while others learn the skills. While it is most common to think about applying management skills in situations where numerous designers and other stakeholders work on a single project, the same competencies are also applicable to solo practice or small studios. Effective management improves designer/client relationships, reduces confusion by articulating objectives for deliverables, and identifies milestones so team members understand where they are in the course of the project.

Managing problems

Even with the best planning and a team of skilled professionals, problems may arise during the creative process. Clients may alter their goals for a project, research can show that agreed objectives do not fit with the expectations of the intended audience, and team members may disagree about the best course of action. It is the manager's job to mitigate problems before they threaten the success of the entire project. The best managers are often known for their ability to react and realign in times of trouble as much as they are for their skill in handling day-to-day situations.

A manager should recognize when there is urgency and be prepared to take action when needed. Sometimes it may be necessary to go back to the client and explain the difficulty and reassess the project's scope and goals. In these instances, the relationship one has developed with the client and team members is key. If the client trusts a manager and can be made to understand how challenges can be addressed, they are more likely to agree to changes or increases in time and/or budget allotted to complete the project. If the goals or intended outcomes of a project are altered once work has begun, then an amendment to the original contract, called a 'change order', will outline revisions. These include listing new activities that have to be performed, new deliverables to be produced and a revised timeline and budget.

4.24 Eco-house

The design of this sustainably built weekend retreat includes the use of reclaimed bricks, tiles and oak decking, a ground source heat pump, extensive use of LED lighting, a photovoltaic array on the sedum roof and hemp insulation.

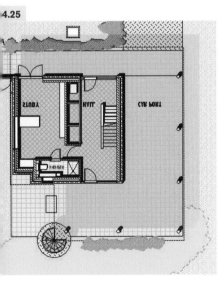

4.25 Forever Green

UK-based ecological architects Forever Green design buildings that use natural materials and work with rather than against nature.

Tools for project management

One of the most important ways a design manager can lay the foundation for a successful outcome is by creating a structure for the activities of the design team. This framework can be used to highlight how the design process will be employed to solve a specific problem and to show the order in which various tasks will be completed. Software systems are often used to record specific tasks, share files and facilitate communication between colleagues.

Project management software can be bought off-the-shelf, as part of a package, or may be customized to the needs of a particular company. These software systems allow the team to see which projects are in progress, including deadlines and milestones. They allow file sharing and include status reports, schedules, billing information, purchase orders, expenses, income projections and contact information.

Giving feedback

It is the job of the design manager to oversee quality control and it is often necessary for a manager to give feedback on visual explorations, roughs and concept drawings before they are presented to clients or higher levels of management. Determining whether work is to a certain standard is usually based on experience, and the manager may need to judge whether or not to proceed in a specific direction.

Learning to effectively critique design work is an essential skill. If design solutions require negative feedback, it is important to be constructive and include alternate ideas or solutions. Tie feedback to stated goals and notice if a person has taken offence. Be specific and list positive attributes, as well as ones that need to be improved. Avoid getting emotional or personal. If criticism is focused and constructive, the person is more likely to successfully make the improvements or changes needed to move a project forward.

Articulating the design process

Chapter 2 outlined opportunities to use design to work beyond the bounds of the project brief and in diverse contexts, and the previous section argued for a broadening of the success criteria for design. To this end, frameworks outlining how and when specific design-related competencies will be employed can be particularly helpful. The development of an articulated process can also be used to align the goals of the project with larger objectives while taking into account how waste, end-of-life, materials-based issues and/or the specifics of an audience or location may affect a project's outcomes.

Creative briefs

Creative briefs (also called design briefs) contain background information about the client and/or project, information about the target audience and competitors, short- and long-term goals and objectives, as well as project-specific details. A brief can act as a work order and should communicate the parameters of a project, as well as the context in which final outputs will have to exist.

A client's brief usually stipulates outcomes for a project, but coming up with and getting a client to sign-off on a set of detailed design-specific goals will help to ensure that both designers and the client agree on an overall direction for a project. Briefs for more broadly defined strategic projects may simply set up the context or define a problem and strategists and/or designers will actively participate in the creation of a more narrowly defined design brief or set of outcome objectives.

The design process in context

In the 1980 edition of *Design Methods*, author John Chris Jones wrote about a shift that was underway from the notion that design should simply facilitate 'progress' to the idea that the 'process' of designing could be an end unto itself. Jones explored how new methods of design problem solving could be put to use to tackle increasingly complex problems and to improve upon traditional design methods. The basis for this hypothesis grew out of a notion that in industrial countries, man-made objects or systems (traffic, airport congestion, road accidents, urban decay, medical treatment, education, etc.) are a failure of design to properly take into account the conditions created by the objects produced for modern life. Jones explained that with this failure comes responsibility. 'The design process (should) become more public so that everyone who is affected by design decisions can foresee what can be done and can influence the choices that are made.'

4.26 Working without a brief

Israeli product designer Yoav Kotik, began his experiment making jewellery without the benefit of a traditional creative brief or a client. Self-initiated work can allow a designer to be more creative and to define their process along the way.

4.27

4.27 Upcycled jewellery

Bottle caps and other raw materials often retain the markers of their previous life and Kotik incorporates these visuals into the design.

4.28 Innovating a process

In Kotik's new line of jewellery the designer changes his process to incorporate the look of precious metal by plating bottle caps in 24-carat gold.

Outline of the design process

- Overview of brief
- Problem definition
- Research and competitive analysis
- Life cycle or end-of-life analysis
- Audience profile
- Evaluation of whether design deserves to exist
- Communication strategy (including goals and objectives)
- Guidelines on tone (visual/verbal)
- Criteria for measuring success
- Visual/conceptual exploration (how the output looks/functions)
- Production (and installation if needed)
- Assessment and evaluation

Improving design processes

Jones suggested that improvements in design processes can be achieved when practitioners use methodologies, including workflow diagrams and flowcharts, which are specifically suited for the problem or tasks at hand. Since the printing of the 1992 edition of *Design Methods*, the predictions about increased complexity suggested by Jones have only been amplified and the use of articulated, and often-customized processes for solving design problems have become the norm.

Creating a rational breakdown of design-related activities is particularly effective in situations where one is not provided with a traditional brief, for large scale projects, and in self-authored work. Life cycle analysis, environmental impacts, end-of-life issues, ethical concerns and local context can all be evaluated during specific phases of the design process, and outlining when these issues will be addressed can help with the organization of resources and personnel. Most importantly, learning to effectively manage the design process will allow practitioners to create successful outcomes that take social and environmental values into account, while helping clients and stakeholders understand how designers achieve preferable results.

4.29

4.29 Research into materials

Like any other design project, Kotik began by researching his material and finding out what it was capable of doing and how best to use it in his designs.

123

4.30	Website manager	Web developer	Content administrator	Web administrator	Sales manager
Project planning	a	r	c	c	c
Website construction	a	r	c	c	i
Content review	i	c	a r	i	i
Usability testing	i	a	c	r	
Installation of tracking software	i	a		r	
Ongoing review of visitors		a		r	i
Sales follow-up to frequent users				i	a r

4.30 RAM

RAM is a framework used in organizing, planning and monitoring the roles and responsibilities of participants in a project or business process.

Responsibility Assignment Matrix

Responsibility Assignment Matrix (RAM) is a system that describes participants by the various roles they perform in completing tasks or creating deliverables for a project. RAM is a useful tool to highlight the roles and responsibilities of various team members in projects where professionals from different disciplines have to work together. Many people may perform a single role and one person may perform many roles. For example, a project manager may be accountable in some instances, responsible in others, and may act as council at other times.

- **Responsible**: Those who do the work to achieve a stated task.

- **Accountable**: The one who is responsible for work having been done, i.e. who has to sign off on a task or deliverable.

- **Council**: Those who provide opinions and specific information; there is typically two-way communication.

- **Informed:** Those who are kept up-to-date on progress, but with whom there is usually only one-way communication.

' The solution to a difficult problem, or the occurrence of an original idea, will often come all of a sudden (the 'leap of insight') and will take the form of a dramatic change in the way in which the problem is perceived. The effect of this transformation is often to turn a complicated problem into a simple one.'
John Chris Jones, designer

Initiating the creative process

Brainstorming and ideation are important parts of the creative process and should be allotted time within any project structure. These methods are particularly useful when working on broader, less-defined problems and may be used to generate ideas about how design can improve the environmental and/or social performance of a product or service. Whether one employs techniques such as mind maps and webbing, or simply uses drawings and associative writing to show rough concepts, brainstorming is a useful way to quickly test initial proposals and to explore a topic with a team.

Once initial ideas have been generated, they should be rated and evaluated against the project's goals and objectives and/or environmental and ethical criteria. Those that do not meet stated objectives should be discarded. What is left can provide the basis for more refined design explorations. At the end of each phase of a project, the team should evaluate whether the findings, explorations or outputs meet the intended goals of the project. This will save time and makes the identification of effective ideas easier.

Working with clients

One of the most important things a professional can do is to educate clients about how designers work. A lack of understanding often forms the basis for resistance to the creative process. Adopting transparent processes and sharing them with stakeholders helps to ensure that clients and non-designers understand how design affects both short- and long-term objectives. Clients can be active participants in the design process if designers define what needs to be accomplished and provide reasons for design decisions.

Designers should avoid missing deadlines or creating work that does not meet the expectations outlined in the brief or exceeds the budget. If there is a problem, tell the client as quickly as possible. Avoid surprises. Compare business or client needs with audience expectations. If there are contradictions between audience needs and the goals of the project, address those concerns immediately. Ensure work is approved at predetermined intervals and update clients on progress and whether or not the project is on schedule.

While a defined process helps managers organize a team's approach to a design problem, effective research and planning will not automatically produce a successful design solution. Sometimes a leap of faith is required. Team members may arrive at a solution that transcends the design brief and creates an outcome that exceeds clients' expectations. Such instances require flexibility and may necessitate explanation to clients or stakeholders about how the proposed output meets the objectives and goals, even if the results are unexpected.

Clients should approve the following:

- Creative or design-specific goals
- Rough concepts
- Preliminary designs
- Revised design solutions
- Final outputs and/or installations

Case study
Elio Studio

Who Creative studio and consultancy

What Design storytelling, writing and brand consultancy

Where London, UK

Why it matters

Flexible collaboration allows professionals from different backgrounds who use articulated organizational methodologies to work together on both client-driven and self-initiated projects.

Flexible collaboration

Elio Studio, a creative studio and consultancy, uses storytelling to inspire businesses and individuals to create positive change. Founder, Leonora Oppenheim is a multidisciplinary designer with a background in working for design studios in the UK, Spain and the Netherlands. The Elio team expands and contracts depending on the scope of a project. Under Oppenheim's direction, a diverse group of designers, architects, writers and engineers may collaborate on a competition, work as consultants, or develop self-initiated projects. Elio Studio uses design storytelling to help forge emotional connections between people and the environment. The studio has three main areas of focus: design is used to craft visual stories; consulting helps communicate brand narratives; and writing, which focuses on highlighting purposeful innovation, is used to package the output created by consulting, and to narrate proposals and competition applications.

Oppenheim's impetus for creating a working model based on ideas rather than products was a reaction to the commoditization of most design outputs. While researching stories for TreeHugger (a media outlet for sustainability), Oppenheim discovered how disconnected people are from how and where products are made. She was amazed at how arbitrary most design decisions are, and how little responsibility designers take in their roles. 'The more I wrote, the more I understood about wastefulness, scarcity, pollution and crazy inefficiencies,' she says. Eventually, Oppenheim could no longer imagine making high-end furniture or consumer products and became interested in finding a way to combine writing and design. She now believes that design can and should be used to work towards Millennium Development Goals and in the service of issues impacting the world.

4.31 Kings Cross, London (UK)

Elio Studio proposed a space (rendered by Chris Haughton) that allowed people to relax and have fun. It was designed to have a different feel from the surrounding environment, but to make the most of its location next to the canal and the heritage structure of the gasholder. The landscaping was influenced by carboniferous forests that contrasted with the modernity of the building.

4.31

4.32

4.32 The Pulse

The design of The Pulse (lead architect Nick Hancock Design Studio) would have sustained itself environmentally through its advanced biomimetic systems, and financially, through a schedule of public and private events and its café franchise. The competition proposal was visually engaging and informative.

Creating solutions

'Collaboration is important because the issues surrounding sustainable innovation are complex,' says Oppenheim. To create the most relevant solutions, she suggests that 'a networked systems approach is needed and the best way to do that is to leave our disciplinary silos and cross pollinate with others.' Not every designer is suited to working in multidisciplinary, less-defined situations. Connectors, translators and managers are needed. To that end, Oppenheim acts like a ringmaster for Elio Studio. Different types of projects require distinct expertise and the number of people working on a job will vary depending on a project's scope, budget and the skill sets needed to produce the intended outputs.

The flexibility of Elio Studio's system allows team members to work on projects they would not be able to undertake on their own, while still giving each individual the time and space to pursue personal work.

Design in context

For an architectural competition sponsored by Kings Cross Central, property developers of a 67-acre complex in central London (UK), Oppenheim and her team created a unique vision of a public and commercial space designed to communicate a historical narrative, while looking towards a future. The project team included designers, architects, illustrators, structural engineers and landscape architects, with each team member playing an integral role in creating the final design and competition proposal.

The *Pulse*, the title of the Elio Studio proposal, was set in Gasholder 8, a space formerly used for a complex system of energy regulation and release. Design elements highlighted the history of energy use and connected viewers to the space's previous function. Patterns were inspired by the sori spores on fern leaves and the kinetic sculpture acts as a roof, capturing rainwater and collecting solar power through photovoltaic films. Unfortunately, The *Pulse* proposal did not win the Kings Cross competition, but Oppenheim remains enthusiastic about the project and feels that one unrealized project may lead to new opportunities.

4.33

4.34

4.33–4.34 Petal flyer

Participants chose a petal and wrote down what they thought they were best at. Then they attached it to the sculpture. 'Petals' built up slowly over two weeks and made the sculpture – which represented *One Planet Living* – change and appear fuller by the end of the event.

One Planet Living

An Elio Studio working group can shrink all the way down to one person if the specifications of a project do not necessitate a larger team. BioRegional, a social enterprise, devised *One Planet Living* (OPL). Oppenheim was commissioned by them to design an exhibition stand at The Garden Party to Make a Difference, as part of the Prince of Wales's Start initiative. The goal for the space was to illustrate ten principles of *One Planet Living*, to influence behavioural change in viewers/participants, and to connect with like-minded business owners. The resulting installation and exhibition included several interactive elements and games. In the simplest interaction, a pin badge of the *One Planet* logo was handed out to festival-goers to wear. Repeatedly seeing the event logo created a moving symbol of OPL at The Garden Party.

Another interaction was based on a sculpture, which evolved over the course of the event with the addition of participant feedback. Oppenheim also created wallpaper that illustrated how many of the planet's resources are used on different continents. Posters showed the ten OPL principles.

Connections through data

For Elio Studio's *Creative Data* initiative, Oppenheim was inspired by sustainable consultancies like Beyond Green, a UK-based company that helps clients to plan, design, build and manage beautiful, long-lasting sustainable environments. Many consultancies create detailed reports that do not always result in actual implementation. This became the impetus for Oppenheim to use design in order to give visual form to complicated information and statistics.

Creative Data is a long series of installations designed to produce innovative and engaging ways of communicating data and research. Its strength is its ability to bring together stakeholders who otherwise might not collaborate with each other. Projects take inspiration from environmental, social and material studies and are driven by a replicable model that includes research, installation and education.

Creative Data works as a mediator between scientists and the public. It seeks to help climate science transition from its reliance on popular images, such as polar bears stuck on the ice cap, to a more nuanced and applicable view of climate change.

4.35

4.36

The Butterfly Effect

For the *Butterfly Effect,* the pilot project in the *Creative Data* series, Elio Studio collaborated with climate and social scientists at the University of East Anglia. The goal was to use creative manifestations of the scientists' work to spark a dialogue with the local community about the future of the Norfolk and Suffolk Broads (see page 130). Using Paul Munday's PhD thesis 'Visualizing Future Wetland Landscapes' as a starting point, the concept of changing land use in the Broads and its relationship to future socio-economic scenarios and climate change were investigated. The resulting installation, which took place at the Sustainable Living Festival in Norwich's Forum (UK), was a visually powerful interactive exhibit. Various designed outputs and educational materials invited visitors to explore their own views on the future of the Broads' environment.

4.36 Creative Data

A large map of the Broads connects viewers to an environment with which they are already familiar.

4.35 Installation

The *One Planet Living* installation uses graphics to inform the public and to reveal data; at the same time, interactive elements invite participation.

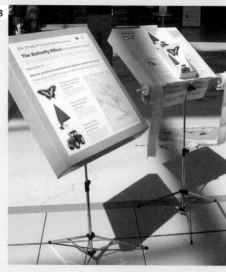

4.37 Map of the Broads

The public were invited to contribute to a map of the Broads using stickers that represented different land uses. The map evolved daily as more and more stickers were added, creating a real time butterfly effect over the course of one week.

Good For Nothing

Good For Nothing is the social mission of the Pipeline Project, an innovation consultancy focused on social and environmental challenges. Through drop-in sessions and collaborative workshops people donate time and money to support others trying to make positive changes (see www. goodfornothing.com).

The Broads

The Broads are a network of mostly navigable rivers and lakes in the English counties of Norfolk and Suffolk. They make up Britain's largest protected wetland and are home to some of the rarest plants and animals in the UK.

Entrepreneurship

Creative Data has been funded through a combination of public and private sources, and Oppenheim says fund-raising is one of the biggest challenges she faces when trying to expand the initiative. Oppenheim is interested in monetizing the learning and outputs created during the first iteration of the project. She plans to produce course packets and other educational materials, which could be used to fund new forms of the project.

When outputs are motivated by ethics as well as profits, the path taken by entrepreneurs may be non-traditional. For example, hiring someone to work on fund-raising or who has experience of selling to the educational market may be more important than securing permanent offices or employing additional designers.

Facilitating a repeatable process

Good for Nothing is an example of how a problem-solving process can be repeated with consistently strong results. A division of the Pipeline Project (see www.pipelineproject.co), Good for Nothing events act like a creative think tank on super drive. They bring together individuals from various backgrounds who donate their time to work on three creative strategy briefs submitted by non-profit groups. Participants choose the project they would prefer to work on and spend 48 hours creating an 'emergency response' to problems outlined in the briefs.

Oppenheim, who is a key participant in The Pipeline Project sessions, points out how working with such a wide range of professionals allows team members to learn about other businesses and gain valuable experience. In one scenario, participants may develop a branding strategy and rewrite an organization's mission statement, while another team might identify ways in which a non-profit organization can tap into new revenue streams. Good For Nothing is successful because the event revolves around a working process rather than predetermined outcomes. This allows the context and objectives to change at the same time as new participants join. A constant flux might be a hindrance in a more traditional workplace, but it is the lifeblood of Good For Nothing and is proof that non-traditional systems can be used to respond to a range of problems.

4.39

4.38–4.39 Creative projects

Elio Studio worked with local education authorities, teachers and children to develop creative projects that help disseminate the project themes into the local community.

The challenges of collaboration

Elio Studio's loose structure has benefits, such as low overheads and flexibility, but there are challenges as well. Oppenheim admits that it is sometimes difficult to keep up momentum when everyone works in different geographic locations. She is the driving force of project management and needs to be totally committed to producing results. Also, since some projects are self-initiated, it can take a long time to find funding and get started.

Stakeholders and collaborators may have different working styles or understandings of what is expected. For example, the *Butterfly Effect* partnered with school personnel who had little experience of working online. Simply getting teachers to reply to emails proved difficult and Oppenheim had to adjust her expectations and the pace of the project to match the realities on the ground.

On the other hand, if team members have similar working styles, collaboration can be effortless, as was the case with geographer, Lucy Rose, who worked on *Creative Data's* engagement strategy. Using Skype meant that communicating was easy even though Rose was in Cornwall (in south-west England) and Oppenheim was in London. 'We would Skype each other at least once a week and then make plans to catch up in person every few months.'

The diversity of Elio Studio's collaborators may sometimes require that special attention is paid to project management. However, the benefit of working with professionals from diverse backgrounds more than makes up for any difficulties encountered. It is this influx of fresh ideas that enables Oppenheim and her team to tackle projects that are beyond the traditional purview of designers.

4.40

4.41

4.40–4.41 The Butterfly Effect

Education packs and workshops use the materials from the *Butterfly Effect* installation to disseminate the project into the local community. Networking among schools enhanced the educational outreach of the project. Schools came together to create a final exhibition that demonstrated the value of learning resulting from the project.

Activity: One Planet Living

In the previous case study, Leonora Oppenheim designed an exhibition booth, which highlighted the ten principles of One Planet Living at a garden party. One Planet Living uses ecological foot printing as its key indicator of sustainability and promotes the idea that living sustainably should mean a better quality of life. For this activity, create a customized display or interactive activity/game designed to help people in your community understand the importance of the OPL principles.

Part A: Design

01 Research the ten principles of *One Planet Living* and why they are important. Begin by visiting www.oneplanetliving.org and www.oneplanetliving.net. Read about the communities and companies who use the OPL model to reduce their environmental impact and demonstrate their commitment to sustainability.

02 Teach the OPL principles to a particular age group or segment of the population within your local community. For instance, an interactive activity may target school-age children, whereas an exhibition booth or display at a local government office or in a public space may be aimed at working adults.

03 Create a visual language to make the ten principles more engaging (you may focus specifically on principles that you think will have particular resonance in your location or with your target audience).

04 Sketch how a visual display might present information to the public or how an interaction/game will engage users.

05 Show your design proposal to a colleague or classmate for feedback.

06 Create a 3D rendering (for a display) or a mock-up of the interaction/game.

Part B: Outreach

07 Make a list of five or more physical locations or local community groups who could use your interaction or display.

08 Contact non-profits, schools or divisions of local government to see if they might be willing to exhibit the display you have created, or test the interaction with a group of students.

09 If possible, exhibit your display and interview viewers for feedback. Similarly, you can test the interaction/game with members of the target audience. Find out if your design is effective and whether the audience is more or less interested in OPL principles because of your work.

Global challenge	OPL principle	OPL goal and strategy
Climate change due to build-up of carbon dioxide (CO_2) in the atmosphere.	**Zero carbon**	**Achieve net CO_2 emissions of zero from OPL developments** Implement energy efficiency in buildings and infrastructure; supply energy from on-site renewable sources, topped-up by new off-site renewable supply.
Waste from discarded products and packaging create, a huge disposal challenge, while squandering valuable resources.	**Zero waste**	**Eliminate waste flows to landfill and for incineration** Reduce waste generation through improved design; encourage reuse, recycling and composting; generate energy from waste cleanly; eliminate the concept of waste as part of a resource-efficient society.
Travel by car and plane can cause climate change, air and noise pollution, and congestion.	**Sustainable transport**	**Reduce reliance on private vehicles and achieve major reductions of CO_2 emissions from transport** Provide transport systems that reduce dependence on fossil fuel use. Offset carbon emissions from air and car travel.
Destructive patterns of resource exploitation and use of non-local materials in construction and manufacture increase environmental harm and reduce gains to the local economy.	**Local and sustainable materials**	**Transform materials supply to the point where it has a net positive impact on the environment and local economy** Where possible, use local, reclaimed, renewable and recycled materials in construction and products, these minimize transport emissions, spur investment in local natural resource stocks and boost the local economy.
Industrial agriculture produces food of uncertain quality and harms local ecosystems, while consumption of non-local food imposes high transport impacts.	**Local and sustainable food**	**Transform food supply to the point where it has a net positive impact on the environment, local economy and people's well-being** Support local and low-impact food production that provides quality food while boosting the local economy in an environmentally beneficial manner; showcase low-impact packaging, processing and disposal; highlight benefits of a low-impact diet.
Local freshwater supplies are often insufficient to meet human needs due to pollution, disruption of hydrological cycles and depletion of existing stocks.	**Sustainable water**	**Achieve a positive impact on local water resources and supply** Implement water-use efficiency measures, reuse and recycling; minimize water extraction and pollution; foster sustainable water and sewage management in the landscape; restore natural water cycles.
Loss of biodiversity and habitats due to development in natural areas and overexploitation of natural resources.	**Natural habitats and wildlife**	**Regenerate degraded environments and halt biodiversity loss** Protect or regenerate existing natural environments and the habitats they provide to fauna and flora; create new habitats.
Local cultural heritage is being lost throughout the world due to globalization, resulting in a loss of local identity and wisdom.	**Culture and heritage**	**Protect and build on local cultural heritage and diversity** Celebrate and revive cultural heritage and local and regional identity; choose structures and systems that build on this heritage; foster a new culture of sustainability.
Some in the industrialized world live in relative poverty, while many in the emerging economies cannot meet their basic needs from what they produce or sell.	**Equity and fair trade**	**Ensure that the OPL community's impact on other communities is positive** Promote equity and fair trading relationships to ensure that the OPL community has a beneficial impact on other communities both locally and globally, notably disadvantaged communities.

5.1 Fair trade rug

This rug was designed by Chris
Haughton and woven in Nepal
using fair trade principles.

CHAPTER 05

Envisioning Sustainable Systems

Examining how contemporary practitioners produce ethically-driven and human-centred outputs can reveal methods and ideas that can be applied to one's own professional practice and in situations where one has to take a leadership role.

The designers, activists, marketers and companies featured in this chapter exemplify how design thinking, marketing skills, and advances in materials applications and technology, can provide the impetus for change, while also highlighting the difficulties faced by ethically motivated designers and companies. Readers are encouraged to consider how they would tackle the problems presented in the following case studies. While doing so, it is also important to ask whether some solutions have been overlooked, as well as to evaluate whether the working models detailed here could be applied in new locations and to different market sectors.

5.2 Concept car

The environmental attributes of this concept car are supplemented by an emotionally appealing design.

When being the best is not enough

Eco-Products is the largest trade show of environmentally preferable products and services in the world. It is held at Tokyo Big Site, an enormous convention and exhibition space in downtown Tokyo, Japan. The size of the exhibition space and the show's ability to draw thousands of visitors each year is a testament to how far the movement toward sustainable products and services has come during the last decade. It also underscores how much more interested the Japanese public is in new products and eco-friendly solutions than many of their counterparts in other countries. Eco-Products is a place to explore, to meet like-minded professionals, to see recently developed innovations and the market challenges faced by companies producing sustainable or eco-friendly products.

Hundreds of booths display materials, products, services and sometimes, even just ideas. It is easy to say that collaboration results in outputs that are greater than the sum of each contributor's part, but in the exhibit halls of Eco-Products, that idea was played out over and over again. In such a frenetic space, it is possible that visitors overlook the single greatest improvement or offer, not because of its lack of applicability, but simply because it needed effective marketing and communication design.

Eco-Products can be seen as a scaled down model of the global marketplace. It is not enough to come up with the next big thing, great idea, or technical innovation. In order to achieve market penetration, ethically-driven outputs need to be backed by sound business principles and effective messaging.

5.3 Infographics

It can be difficult to understand the attributes of some environmentally preferable products. This infographic gives viewers information by combining text and imagery.

5.4 Mobile phones

Mobile technology can be used to convey information, facilitate trade and empower local populations.

Avoiding other's mistakes

Similarities between Japan, the world's third largest economy, and the US, the world's largest, abound. One can go to McDonald's, drink Coca-Cola, and buy US brands as readily in Tokyo as in New York. Similarly, Japanese exports to the US and Europe, such as Toyota cars and Sony electronics, are ubiquitous. Even Japanese food, mostly in the form of sushi, has a loyal following of American and European enthusiasts. However, despite scores of motivated designers, activists and business people, neither the world's first nor third largest economy has figured out how to successfully tackle the problem of diminishing resources and increasing demand for consumable products. However, in each case, one culture can learn from the other.

Innovation driving sustainable solutions

Sustainable product designer and professor at Tokyo Zokei University, Fumikazu Masuda has suggested that with limitation, there is also opportunity. He believes that China and other emerging economies can learn from the mistakes developed countries have made by leapfrogging over their wasteful systems and clunky technologies, and implementing more elegant solutions. If that advice seems far-fetched, it is useful to remember that this is exactly what has happened with telecommunications in most of the developing world. Mobile technology has exploded in countries that never fully adopted the wired infrastructure needed for landline phones.

Cell/mobile phones have penetrated almost every part of the world today. In many parts of Africa, where Internet access is non-existent and power is intermittent, cell technology has given people the power to communicate, to access information and to conduct commerce. If the same approach can be used for transportation, entertainment and energy usage, the question becomes how to implement the smartest, most innovative solutions within national boundaries rather than whether or not countries should seek further development. Following this logic, the donation of thousands of cheap computers to children in the developing world may be generous, but a misguided use of resources.

If we consider the dual goals of dematerialization and increased functionality, a more elegantly designed solution could be found in a new generation of mobile or hand-held technology that allows for greater functionality, lower costs and environmentally sensitive manufacturing. Using existing infrastructure and creating solutions that are tailored to a particular environment can produce greater gains than one country just adopting the practices of another.

137

Case study
Project Masiluleke

Consumption

Fair Trade

Materials

New markets

Problem solving

Production

Storytelling

Technology

Who iTeach, frog design, Praekelt and partners that include foundations, corporations, NGOs and health care representatives

What Project using mobile phones as a high-impact, low-cost means of delivering health care information and connecting populations in need to existing services

Where South Africa

Why it matters

With HIV/AIDS creating an escalating worldwide health crisis, efficient and cost effective solutions are needed. The use of mobile technology can provide low-cost innovative solutions that can be used in locations throughout the world.

PopTech

Born at PopTech, an ideas summit and social innovation network, Project Masiluleke (Project M) is a collaborative effort using mobile technology to help reverse the HIV/AIDS and tuberculosis (TB) crisis in South Africa. The project uses mobile phones as a high-impact, low-cost means of delivering health care information and connecting populations to existing services. In its second phase, the project is piloting a solution for HIV self-testing kits that are linked to health care services through users' mobile phones.

A helping hand

Project Masiluleke (*masiluleke* means 'to give wise counsel' and to 'lend a helping hand' in Zulu) has brought together a diverse group of partners with the goal of reducing the spread of HIV/AIDS and TB.

The statistics are overwhelming, with more than 40 per cent of the population infected in some provinces. HIV related illnesses kill about 270,00 people a year in South Africa, and connecting them with health care is an issue of great importance.

The country has nearly 100 per cent mobile phone penetration, so using mobile technology offers health care providers a valuable tool for providing information, conducting outreach and maintaining contact with their patients.

Many people who qualify for anti-retroviral (ARV) drugs do not receive them. The stigma against those living with HIV keeps many people from being tested until they are symptomatic with end-stage AIDS. The goal of Project M is to help people determine their status and to connect them with treatment earlier in the illness.

'Project M demonstrates the power that mobile technology has to address some of the big issues facing the world today.'
Anthony Darcy,
Project Coordinator,
Nokia Siemens Networks

5.5

5.6

5.5–5.6 Self-testing kits

Project M includes self-testing kits (like those currently available in developed counties) so people can find out their status in the privacy of their own home.

Mobile access

Nearly all of South Africa's population (including the young and the poor) has mobile phone access. Therefore, mobile phones can be cost-effectively used to:

- Close the health care 'information gap' by delivering geographically and culturally appropriate messages that encourage people to learn their HIV status earlier.

- Connect people to existing 'on-the-ground' HIV and TB clinical services for testing and treatment.

- Increase people's adherence to AVR regimens once in treatment.

5.7

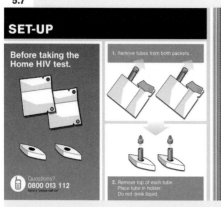

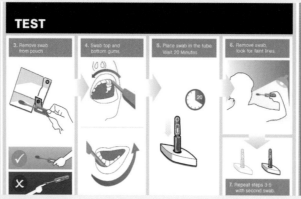

5.7 Importance of design

Self-testing kits include easy to
understand instructions that use
illustrations and minimal text.
This allows users who may have
different levels of education to
successfully use the tests.

Using mobile technology for outreach

Based on the system of the home
pregnancy test, free HIV self-testing
kits were designed by frog design and
iTeach. The kits are designed to be easy
to use and come with information and
instructions in local languages. Users
connect to health care support via a
mobile phone.

For patients who are already on AVR
drugs, a system called TxtAlert sends
SMS reminders to schedule clinic visits,
which helps to ensure that patients stick
to their medical regimes. 'With Project M,
we are seeing the powerful impact that
mobile technologies can have in raising
awareness of serious health issues
and encouraging positive behaviour
change on a massive scale,' says Robert
Fabricant, Vice President of Creative for
frog design. 'This potential will not be
realized without the direct application of
design to ensure that these services are
simple and human.'

'Please Call Me'

Created as a seed project, all
components developed for Project M
are open source and are designed to
be replicated worldwide without the
need for licenses. While the statistics
on the numbers of people living with
HIV/AIDS can be overwhelming, the
use of 'Please Call Me' (PCM) text
messages by Project M has already
helped to triple the average daily call
volume to the National AIDS Helpline in
Johannesburg. Assuming only 2 per cent
of PCM recipients respond in the coming
year – and only half of those initiate
an HIV/AIDS test – Project M has the
potential to mobilize several hundred
thousand South Africans to get tested
on an annual basis.

Project M collaborators

The list of collaborators
participating in Project M is
impressive and includes iTeach,
the Praekelt Foundation, frog
design, MTN, Nokia Siemens
Networks, Ghetto Ruff, National
Geographic Society, LifeLine
Southern Africa, Children
of South African Legacies,
and World-Class Advisors.

Activity: Mobile technology campaign

Mobile phone subscriptions have now reached 4.6 billion, and in less than a decade, subscription rates have doubled in the developing world. This means mobile technology is one of the best ways to reach diverse populations at low cost.

(Note: The rates for sending and receiving text messages vary depending on the country and the provider, so for any mobile phone-based campaign, the cost needs to be calculated and included.)

Part A: Thinking and research

01	Consider how mobile technology can be used to combat economic, social and environmental issues. Find more examples like Project M and make a list.
02	Choose a health care related social cause, and then decide on a location to target, either in your community or internationally. Research how current outreach is conducted and consider the context in which your solution would be applied.
03	Make a list of the most pressing considerations affecting populations that are impacted by your 'cause'.
04	Consider how mobile technology might be used in service of the cause and make a list of challenges your plan might face.

Part B: Visual solutions

05	For visual communication designers, advertisers and marketers – create an identity for your campaign. Expand your campaign with design solutions that combine the more traditional outputs of a public service campaign with your mobile phone outreach plan, e.g. brochures, billboards, posters or websites.
06	For product designers – consider how existing products can be improved and how new technology and products might help with an outreach campaign to provide services. Create concept drawings of product innovations or improvements.
07	Collate your research and ideas into a campaign report.

Efficiency

Innovation

New markets

Problem solving

Storytelling

Technology

Case study
1 in 29

Who Information designer Sidhika Sooklal

What Public awareness campaign

Where South Africa

Why it matters

Sidhika Sooklal has created a prototype public awareness campaign that targets the South African women at risk of developing cervical cancer.

Public awareness campaign

South African designer Sidhika Sooklal has employed some of the same techniques used by Project Masiluleke in her public awareness campaign, 1 in 29. Sooklal's campaign is currently in the concept phase – she is looking for sponsors and donors to pay for programmes and research.

Inspired by the stark reality that cervical cancer affects women in the developing world four times more frequently than those living in industrialized countries, Sooklal's work is targeted at the women whose lives are most at risk. Based on the success of similar campaigns that inform women at risk of breast cancer, Sooklal would focus on several areas. She will inform women about cervical cancer and the benefits of early detection through brochures, postcards and informational diagrams; and like Project M, she plans to use mobile phone technology to connect to patients and to give test results. She offers a solution to the problem of inconvenient or distant testing facilities through the use of mobile health units.

Sooklal's campaign is a call to action with a simple objective — to promote awareness and educate South African women about the dangers of cervical cancer. Women in the US, Europe, and Japan routinely get screened for cervical cancer. Unfortunately, pap smears (also known as cervical smears), are less common in the developing world where 80 per cent of cases occur. The fact that cervical cancer occurs four times more frequently among black women is an example of how inequity in access to health care can combine with genetic predisposition to create a real health crisis.

5.8

5.9

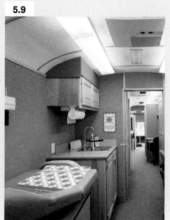

5.8–5.9 Branding and outreach

Branding is an important part of Sooklal's plan for how to outreach to women. Her campaign includes plans to put information about cervical cancer and the importance of screening in public rest rooms and clinics. These materials would be designed to have a unified visual appearance.

5.10

5.10 Mobile clinics

In addition to outreach via mobile phone messages and
a public service campaign, 1 in 29 includes plans for mobile
clinics, where women living in rural areas could go for
cervical cancer screening and health care counselling.

Design in context

Sooklal's identity for 1 in 29 is a dot
surrounded by 28 female figures. 'The
structure of the symbol serves as a
metaphor for community and the idea of
shared networked information,' she says.
It can be used in combination to create a
pattern that enhances the informational
materials, while providing a distinctive
visual representation.

Campaign materials would be located
in places frequented by women, such as
dressing rooms and bathrooms. The
goal is to create non-threatening
informative messages.

The identity icon and messages would
also appear on popular products and
in the pages of women's magazines.
Sooklal would like the 1 in 29 visual
symbol to be become familiar to women
and to become a first step toward
understanding the disease and a cultural
acceptance of testing.

1 in 29 targets urban populations first,
but since a large percentage live in
rural areas, Sooklal has included mobile
health care clinics to extend the reach
of the campaign. These clinics could
travel to areas where women would
otherwise be cut-off from health care
and where information about the disease
and testing is scarce. These clinics
would create a ripple effect by using
ambassadors who would be chosen from
local communities to act as educators
and participate in outreach.

Additionally, SMS/MMS notification
systems and postcards with information
about tests would be sent to women who
had received services at mobile clinics.
Connecting patients with information
remotely would mean that women would
not have to travel to receive test results,
and the system would also provide a
means of ongoing communication.
SMS/MMS messages could be sent to
patients to remind them to schedule new
appointments or follow-up visits at the
mobile clinic.

5.11

5.11 Upcycled furniture

British designer Zoe Murphy
prints on recycled furniture
and textiles using imagery
that is inspired by the seaside
town of Margate in Kent (UK).

New frontiers in recycling

There are numerous examples of how
recycling works in contemporary society.
However, two methods have significant
applicability to business strategy and
design thinking. In the first, an item is
reused or remade in such a way that
the new product is not immediately
identifiable as having been made from
repurposed materials. Aluminium cans,
soda bottles and copy paper are all
examples of popular consumer goods,
which look the same regardless of
whether or not they are made from
reused materials. This 'invisible recycling'
can be a benefit to the companies
making products because buying
waste or discarded items may be less
expensive than sourcing raw materials.
Sometimes, the final product may
not even have been marketed as
using reused waste, while at other
times a manufacture, will share
information about the use of
recycled content with consumers.

The second type of recycled product
is often marketed using particular
attributes associated with their
production or with the material from
which they originate. For example,
some products may be produced with
reclaimed or salvaged materials and will
appeal to buyers who are interested in
goods with an antique, handmade or
retro aesthetic, regardless of whether
the buyer cares about the environmental
qualities of the product. This type of
repurposing prolongs the life of a
given material. Artists, designers and
craftspeople often produce objects in
limited number or as unique pieces.

Problems with recycling

Even though recycling household trash is the law in many municipalities and the concept is a popular topic in the media, recycling is not without detractors. In *Cradle to Cradle: Remaking the Way We Make Things* (North Point Press, 2002), authors William McDonough and Michael Braungart present the not-so-positive side of recycling. They suggested that recycling, as it is currently defined, most often results in a 'down cycling' of materials, meaning that when production criteria and systems do not allow for efficient reuse, materials end up degrading and eventually cannot be used again. To McDonough and Braungart, current recycling systems simply prolong the inevitable trip to the landfill. Certainly, structures where waste becomes a 'nutrient' in closed-loop systems are ideal, but we need solutions that solve problems today as well as those that will create substantive change for the future.

As McDonough and Braungart suggest, recycling does not do enough to interrupt the current model of consumption in industrialized countries (which is predicated on the availability of cheap disposable goods). However, while their critique is not inaccurate, it fails to take into account how it can be part of incremental improvements.

Recycling extends the life of objects, and may even double or triple the time a material or object stays in use (and therefore out of landfills). By no means should designers and producers stop looking for better solutions or for materials that can infinitely be reused without degradation, but in the meantime, recycling can provide the impetus for creative individuals, companies and producers to make products a little less 'bad'.

5.12

5.13

5.12–5.13
Recycled and custom tableware
Designer Lou Rota creates custom tableware by reusing vintage plates and adding fanciful designs. The designs of these plates make old dishes feel modern.

Recycling and the mineral industry

Imagine if every company contributed to the good of humanity and the health of the planet – even businesses that specialize in resource extraction and mineral rights. Such organizations are rarely associated with environmental preservation or social change, but some companies are redefining the idea of raw materials to include discarded items and waste products. As the following case study explores, Maruishi Ceramics Materials Company Ltd is pioneering the use of ceramic waste material. Such innovation is prescient, considering the fact that the world's supply of raw materials is finite and discarded items can usually be obtained for little or no cost. Ideally, recycling can be used to help drive innovation and generate revenue as well as an opportunity to 'do good.'

Case study
Redefining raw
materials

Who Maruishi Ceramics Materials
Company Ltd

What Recycled ceramics

Where Seto, Japan

Why it matters

The usable material made by recycling
dishes and plates can keep thousands
of pounds of discarded ceramics out of
landfills and provide a new source of
'raw material' for the company.

Efficiency

Innovation

Materials

New markets

Problem solving

Production

Reuse/Recycling

Technology

5.14 Maruishi site
Maruishi has historically
been known as a company
specializing in mineral
extraction. Here the company
extracts minerals used for
commercial clay production.

Maruishi Ceramics

Located in Seto, Japan, Maruishi Ceramics
is challenging the notion that mineral
extraction and refinement is an industry that
is incompatible with values-based business
practices. Partnering with municipalities
and working with local populations,
the company strives to create practical
applications for a closed-loop system of
ceramic manufacture and processing, a sort
of 'reincarnation' for used pottery.

Home to Seto ware and the Japanese
version of the tenmoku tea bowl, Seto has
been an epicentre for ceramic production
for centuries. Streets are lined with pottery
studios and shops specializing in ceramic
wares and cottage industries are still
thriving. It is a place tourists come to buy
tea bowls and dishes from local artisans
and larger manufacturers alike. The clay
around Seto lacks iron and looks white. It
is so highly prized that the Japanese word
for pottery and porcelain, *setomoro*, literally
means 'things from Seto.'

5.15

5.16

Re-Seto recycling

Maruishi Ceramics was founded in 1874 and first specialized in the production and sale of ceramic wares. After World War II, the company started to produce raw materials for use in large-scale ceramic production.

Today, the company has created a system to recycle used ceramics. The programme, known as 'Re-Seto', develops new recycled ceramic products using waste pottery and porcelain that would otherwise be discarded as non-flammable rubbish and buried in landfills. The prefix 'Re' comes from the three 'Rs': reduce, reuse and recycle, and the use of the city name 'Seto' locates the programme within a long history of innovation of ceramic products and mineral usage.

Maruishi Ceramics has a goal of adding new value and taking advantage of their existing expertise to help address problems that effect municipalities and the local population.

In 2004, Seto citizens began to bring their unused and broken ceramics to their local resource recycling station. People separate porcelain from other pottery so that Maruishi Ceramics could collect the waste ceramics in large woven bags.

The dishes and other ceramic wares are pulverized and then go through a patented process that removes the metals and other colourants used in glazes and other finishes. Mixed with water and shaped into round disks, the 'recycled' clay is used in combination with raw or virgin clay to make new ceramic objects. To expand collection, several other cities in Aichi Province have added ceramic waste collection bins to those that are currently used to collect old and unused clothing.

The finished recycled material has been used to make dishes and public drinking fountains, and the company is exploring other applications for the material.

5.15–5.16 Recycling ceramics

Thousands of unused, often unbroken, dishes in bags and piles at Maruishi Ceramics highlight how many items in good condition are discarded due to their owners' changing tastes.

5.17

5.17 Wares from Maruishi

Wares made from recycled clay material at the Maruishi Ceramics Materials factory.

Benefits of recycling

The benefits of the Re-Seto ceramic recycling programme are three-fold. First, the system keeps solid waste out of landfills and provides a new life for already fired clay material. Secondly, it decreases the cost to municipalities of burying trash, a cost that is significant in a country such as Japan, which has little unused land. Lastly, the process, which adds recycled material to new clay at percentages as high as 50 per cent, means the firing temperature can be decreased from 1300–1200 degrees Celsius. A difference of 100 degrees Celsius may seem small, but when applied to large-scale production it can represent a 20 to 30 per cent saving in energy. Locally, the Re-Seto process and Maruishi Ceramics Materials has used 40 tons of reused ceramic material with plans to expand. The company predicts that if the programme were rolled out nationally, it could result in 140,000 tons of material recovered annually.

By treating waste as a raw material and a potential revenue generator, Maruishi Ceramics Materials is able to innovate their business, serve the local community and keep waste material out of overflowing landfills. By using fewer natural resources, the Re-Seto manufacturing process decreases the environmental load of ceramic manufacturing.

Recycling versus upcycling

Maruishi Ceramics wants to create a closed-loop system for ceramic production, and while certainly laudable, that goal may be unrealistic given current production methods. For now, recycling programmes like the ones being developed by Maruishi Ceramics prolong the useful life of the materials they target. If this kind of 'recycling' increases the applications for a given material and prolongs its life, it is certainly better than our current system where consumers buy and dump and buy again in an endlessly unsustainable cycle. Those companies creating ways to improve materials processing may not be perfect, but they are making a significant contribution by creating more innovative ways of dealing with the waste that is a by-product of industrialized society.

5.18

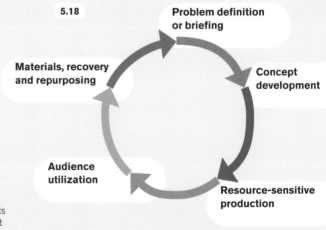

Problem definition or briefing

Concept development

Resource-sensitive production

Audience utilization

Materials, recovery and repurposing

5.18 Life cycle loop: waste as a resource

Applying cradle-to-cradle principles to the design process results in a continuous cyclical use and reuse of resources. Waste is not recycled, but instead is initially produced to transition into becoming a nutrient for new products and materials.

5.19

5.19 Recycled clay

Disks of recycled clay
waiting to be tested
before being formed into
new products.

Where the design comes in

The system developed by Maruishi
Ceramics Materials is a clear
improvement over burying ceramic
waste, but there are still a host of
challenges when recycling ceramics.
Collection and transportation can be
difficult and requires a population that
is prepared to sort waste. Currently, the
'clay' generated from recycled ceramics
is not as strong as virgin material. And,
perhaps most importantly, Maruishi
Ceramic is still experimenting to
find the ideal applications for the
material they have created. This is
where design thinking and problem
solving could be used to identify and
develop solutions for efficiently utilizing
the recycled clay. Residencies for
industrial engineers and designers
could provide opportunities for recent
college graduates, and a wealth of
innovative solutions for companies
such as Maruishi Ceramics. What could
be more exciting for a young designer
or engineer than having free reign at a
working company?

Artists-in-residence programme

An example of one such collaboration is the
artists-in-residence programme that provides
opportunities for visual artists to work with the
Kohler Company in Wisconsin (US). Artists
work in the pottery, iron and brass foundries or
enamel shop and develop original visual work.
Like Kohler, INAX – a company that develops
kitchen and bath fixtures in Japan – has a
residency programme for visual artists.

Strong ties exist between programmes in
higher education and industry in the form of
internships, but expanding these programmes
to include professional designers working in
'think tanks' would provide many solutions.
Would roof tiles or planters be a better use
of the recycled low fire clay? Does it have
application for crafts or hobbyists?

Collaboration and partnerships between
designers and industry offer tremendous
possibilities and opportunities. Design thinking
could be used to improve materials' usage
and manufacturing systems, while creating
products and services that meet real human
needs. And, since it can be applied in situations
where the outcome is not predetermined,
design thinking has direct applicability to
Maruishi Ceramic's problem of what to do
with the material that was created without a
specific purpose in mind.

Activity: Upcycled design

The previous section detailed ways in
which discarded items or waste material
can be used to make new products.
For this activity, you will create your own
upcycled product by recycling discarded
or previously used objects.

01	Research what types of previously used material is freely available or low cost in your community. For this project, you may purchase items at a second-hand store, find them at a refuse station or local trash collecting facility, or obtain them through sites such as Freecycle (www.freecycle.org).
02	Once you have identified several possible materials, begin making sketches of how to turn them into new and usable products. Consider what you would have to charge for the new product to make production realistic (this is an important consideration even for one-of-a-kind pieces). For instance, Maruishi Ceramics Materials obtained the ceramics used for their 'recycling' programme for free, but making new sweaters or scarves from old sweaters may mean buying used items. Therefore the 'new' product may cost more than if material was obtained for free.
03	Review your sketches and identify which design will be most attractive to customers by showing initial design ideas to potential customers and surveying your target market.
04	If possible, create a finished version of your design. If the design requires more intensive production than you have the facilities for, create two- and three-dimensional renderings of the finished product.

Reframing corporate thinking

The impetus for change can come from a variety of sources. Though it is not always true, smaller companies tend to be more nimble, while larger companies often have more difficulty changing their internal structures and the messages they send external stakeholders. Strong leadership by management may be able to realign business strategy with environmental and social values. Alternatively, pressure from consumers or clients might provide the motivation for policy changes.

Another way to instigate change is through the use of an external consultant. As detailed in chapter 1, large and mid-sized companies often hire consultants to help reframe a company's mandate or to kick-start the adoption of new policies. Consultants can create a framework for how to accomplish a particular set of objectives or they may help a team or group of managers make a transition to a new way of working. They can also be used to assist internal groups when the goal is to transform the structure of an organization.

Making branding meaningful

Duke Stump, the subject of the following case study, is an example of a consultant with a vision so broad he does not fit into any one mould. He is not an expert on sustainability per se, but he believes we need to begin looking at who we really are as citizens, what we are gifted at, and how we can take global issues like food, land, poverty, energy and climate and bring them into the internal conversations that happen at companies.

When this is done, 'it ignites a company's culture and will grow the brand.' And that is Stump's goal. His approach is both human centred and profit driven. He believes you can have great companies that have purpose, that care, and that work from a place of meaning. 'The irony is if you want to create effortless loyalty, then create a company that has values and meaning and see what happens,' Stump says. 'You will have people walking 3,000 miles barefoot to be part of that brand.'

Effective management combined with concrete goals and objectives are certainly needed to put ideas like Stump's into action, but his gift is to come in from the outside and inspire new ways of thinking. Sometimes, this type of external driver is needed to help companies re-imagine their mandate and to create more meaningful branding.

5.20

5.20 Renewable energy

The popularity of renewable energy is directly related to its economic feasibility. Wind and solar power are more popular when the prices of other energy sources are high.

5.21

5.21 Benefits of incentives

Governments can jump start innovation though tax cuts and other policies designed to incentivize early adopters of renewable energy solutions. These policy measures can allow start-ups and small companies to compete more easily in a global market.

151

Case study
A new twist on branding

Collaboration
Problem solving
Storytelling
Strategy

Who Duke Stump

What Marketing and branding

Where New Hampshire, US

Why it matters

Stump is revolutionizing how brands relate to their customers and working to create companies that are better able to serve their customers, while still maintaining a positive bottom line.

Sherpa for humanity

As an evangelist for change, Duke Stump's expertise is in marketing and branding, but his approach is unique and completely unconventional (see www. northstarmanifesto.com). Instead of simply trying to sell a product or promote a company's image, he is obsessed with trying to find ways to understand why untapped potential is, well … untapped. Working as a consultant, he helps companies to create conditions where cultures – both internal and external – flourish. The antithesis of a hard-nosed businessman, Stump would rather be known as a 'sherpa for humanity.' It is a title that may seem a bit vague, but when asked what he actually does, Stump simply says he works 'with brilliant folks who have great ideas and simply need some help climbing the mountain'.

Many companies are still trying to understand the concept of 'green' or sustainability. Stump is an advocate for an even broader approach. He is inspired by Buckminster Fuller's principle to 'widen the lens to see the whole', and suggests that creating change is not really about green or even sustainability, but should focus instead on growing meaningful and relevant relationships. This might seem like heresy to those who have fought for years to get concepts like sustainability or green on the table of boardrooms and mid-sized businesses, but Stump is convinced this new breed of brand behaviours already exists and is showing results.

'At the centre of your being you have the answer. You know who you are and you know what you want.'
Duke Stump, marketeer

5.23

5.22

5.22 Trade show booth

Seventh Generation's trade show booth gives visual form to Stump's marketing vision. By connecting products with environmental stewardship, Seventh Generation has been able to appeal to consumers who share the company's values.

5.23 Geodesic dome by Buckminster Fuller

Buckminster Fuller (1895–1983) was an American inventor, scientist, writer and environmental activist. He believed in doing more with less. Fuller was concerned about humanity's wasteful use of resources and was a proponent of social equity. His ideas on the integration of natural systems and human invention, and his advocacy for environmental issues, have inspired many designers and environmentalists.

Seventh Generation

After nearly 16 years working at Nike, Stump, who was the vice-president of product marketing, left to take a position as chief marketing officer for Seventh Generation. Seventh Generation is an American company that sells eco-friendly household and personal care products. The company is known as a leader in the environmental movement and an advocate for larger change. Stump's time at Seventh Generation was less about traditional marketing than it was about strategically re-conceptualizing what a business should be and do. Many of Stump's ideas and concepts are delivered in the form of questions. He asks what would happen if we were to 'quiet our cleverness and take a step back?' Or, 'What if we reframed, redesigned and rethought?' And he advocates for a holistic approach to problem solving.

At Seventh Generation, Stump was part of a company that was creating a model of what it meant to act responsibly as a corporation. Seventh Generation has won many awards for its environmental policies and eco-friendly products.

Values-based work

While taking a year off from Seventh Generation, Stump began to ask himself what would happen if one could ignite conversations about being profitable at the same time as 'doing the right thing' with mid-sized companies. He wondered what would happen if companies could begin to create ideas where humanity was a part of every decision. More than traditional marketing, Stump seeks to re-imagine the relationship that companies can have with consumers, with their partners, and with the planet. Stump is a proponent of a very radical conception of values-based work. He suggests that as a company, 'our purpose is to optimize the relevance and resonance for those we serve'. And to those sceptics out there, yes, he has found plenty of companies, including Fortune 500 companies, that are interested in hearing about and applying his methods.

Stump looks for clients with which to engage in symbiotic partnerships. He has specific criteria that he uses when considering whether or not to take on new clients.

- First and foremost, they have to be positive, systemic change makers who have a zeal for humanity.

- Second, they have to have a courageous and bold leader who is willing to make glorious mistakes.

- Third, they are generally private entrepreneurial enterprises with less than $200 million (approximately £127 million) in annual revenue. He says, 'This is simply what I feel to be my own sweet spot'.

Stump works with his clients to develop a strategy that draws consumers to a brand and where they are part of a company's internal conversation and external messaging. He says a successful brand has customers who are evangelists for that brand, but will also be constructive critics. He compares his version of the ideal connection between customers and corporations with the relationship between two people. He feels it is all about trust. In Stump's opinion this new breed of behaviour will characterize this century's most successful brands.

Promoting brands with honesty

Businesses spend a huge amount of financial and human capital to avoid making mistakes that might cost the company money or detract from the reputation of the brand. Stump sees this defensive approach as completely antithetical to their ability to create a powerful brand and strong organization. He suggests companies should not only accept the possibility of making missteps along the way, but embrace what he calls 'glorious mistakes.'

This mentality means focusing more on what could be than what is. 'It is a permission slip to play from a place of inspiration versus desperation ... and it is based on the belief that playing it safe is risky,' Stump says. He believes that accepting one's mistakes is ultimately about leading with courage and says 'people do not necessarily want perfection, but they absolutely want honesty'.

Stump comments that during his tenure at Seventh Generation, 'the company made its share of mistakes, but they were honest about them'. Seventh Generation used those mistakes as an opportunity to have both an internal and external dialogue on how to do better in the future, and the company was able to incorporate that learning into a strategy that matched its long-term objectives.

5.24

Inspiration not desperation

As mentioned earlier one of Stump's main tenets is that we should work from a place of inspiration, not desperation. He suggests we should always begin by looking at our core beliefs and attributes. He gives the example of the group working on sustainability at Nike, which found that it had difficulty applying sustainable thinking to an existing corporate culture. Eventually, the group backed up, looked at the big picture, and asked, 'What are we great at already?' They found the answer was performance innovation. They realized by injecting Nike's existing values into the conversation about sustainability, the desirable values they identified could become part of the company's business strategy and genetic code.

Internal business culture

Much of Stump's energy is spent helping companies create strategies and an internal culture that is simple, inspiring and empowering. For Stump, 'companies that have great internal cultures are places where human capital is the best and most valuable capital,' he says. 'The goal is to create meaningful, values-based companies.' This means creating an organization where people are nurtured and not hampered by the boundaries around them. His advice to values-based companies is: 'Before you can save the world you have to look inside.'

Stump's human-centred approach to marketing is definitely non-traditional. However, as environmental and social consciousness have become an increasingly desirable attribute for companies, managers often look to consultants like Stump for unusual and visionary approaches when revising the internal culture of their organizations. The companies that hire Stump may not adopt all of his ideas, but bringing in an outsider can lead to meaningful structural and cultural changes within an organization, and provide innovative frameworks for promoting a positive brand position.

5.24 Eco-friendly products

This catalogue for Seventh Generation uses design to highlight the environmental attributes of products. The visual style used by the graphics complements the design of product packaging.

5.25

5.25 Sali Sasaki

Sali Sasaki is a graphic
designer who works in
international development.

Interview:
Sali Sasaki

*What made you think about how design
could promote social practice?*

In July 1987, a working paper entitled
'Graphic Design for Development'
was submitted by board members of
the International Council of Graphic
Design Associations (ICOGRADA)
to the United Nations Educational,
Scientific and Cultural Organization
(UNESCO), following a four-day seminar
in Nairobi, Kenya. The objectives of the
seminar were to raise awareness of the
contributions that graphic design can
make in improving people's lives and
to increase understanding of graphic
design in international organizations.

*How does the professional world of
design encourage and promote new
social design practices?*

At UNESCO, I concentrated on the role
of graphic design for development and
researched its application in the fields
of general education, public health,
environment, public information and
social responsibility through cultural
traditions, contemporary practices and
the empowerment of future generations
of designers. Design is a creative
methodology that has the ability to
support UNESCO's notion of successful
development, which has been defined
as 'a tradition specific to each culture
combined with the most modern
economic, scientific and technological
resources'. (J. Pérez de Cuéllar, 'Our
Creative Diversity', Introduction, The
World Decade for Cultural Development
1988–97, Paris: UNESCO, 7).

**5.26 Sustainable
development**

The UN's focus on sustainable
development supports the
organization's Millennium
Development Goals, which
include ending poverty and
hunger, access to education,
gender equality, health,
environmental sustainability and
global partnerships.

5.27

5.27 United Nations

Because of its scope, the UN
is able to be a global advocate
for social and environmental
policies.

5.28 Learning about water
This poster uses simple visuals
to show the importance of
water as a natural resource.

What is the connection between graphic design, the UN, and international development?

The relationship between graphic design and the United Nations (UN) started in the spring of 1945, when delegates from 50 Allied nations gathered in San Francisco to finalize the charter of the UN during the United Nations Conference on International Organization. What later became one of the world's most recognizable symbols was presented by Donal McLaughlin and his design team: the official United Nations Emblem, a round depiction of the world's continents on circular lines of latitude and vertical lines of longitude framed by two olive branches.

These past few years, UN programmes and agencies have been focusing on their communication strategies more thoroughly and are involving an increasing number of graphic designers to create efficient communication tools. Successful examples are the UNICEF's brand tool kit and UNFPA's online style guide (see the UNFPA styleguide at www.unfpa.org/styleguide).

How has the UN used graphic design to promote its goals?

Poster designs have been a popular way of combining graphic design with UN goals, and designers have collaborated with numerous organizations.
In 2005, the Japan Graphic Designers Association (JAGDA) launched the Water for Life poster competition in partnership with the UN Information Centre in Tokyo. Poster competitions remain popular as graphic design activities with a social twist.

5.29 United Nations' news

US-based designer Sebastian Bettencourt created this awareness campaign for the United Nations News and Media Division.

What is the cultural value of graphic design?

Graphic design has a cultural dimension that is derived from traditions, ethnicity, diversity, languages, gender, beliefs, value systems and a certain ability to 'transform the visual heritage of places and peoples into contemporary commercial currency and cultural expression' (E. Campbell, Design and Architecture Newsletter, London: British Council, 3, 2006). The strength of graphic design lies in its ability to disseminate cultures and in its capacity to make knowledge accessible.

What is the importance of local culture in a globalized world?

In contemporary China, young designers are taking their country to a new creative era, while government officials and businesses see increasing opportunities arising from the 'Designed in China' concept. Hong Kong-based designer Javin Mo is the editor of *3030 New Graphic Design in China*, a publication that features 30 designers from mainland China. It reveals the creative outburst triggered by the rapid economic development and recent social transformations in the country. Through the work of its designers, China has become involved in a global conversation that invests heavily in contemporary culture and creativity. The blend of traditions, ideologies and pop culture that characterizes Chinese visual expression of the twenty-first century could soon turn design into the nation's biggest export.

5.30 Afrikan Alphabets by Saki Mafundikwa

A native of Zimbabwe, Saki Mafundikwa worked as a designer in New York before returning to that country to open a school for graphic design and new media. *Afrikan Alphabets* includes graphics and illustrations as well as text about writing systems from across the African continent.

How can design be used to highlight cultural traditions?

There are many examples of how design works with cultural traditions. For example, after receiving his master's degree in graphic design from Yale University, Saki Mafundikwa returned to Zimbabwe and researched the origins of African writing systems and typography. His research of ten years led to the publication of *Afrikan Alphabets: The Story of Writing in Afrika* (Mark Batty Publisher, 2007). Through a designer's perspective, the book reveals a dimension of African culture that was long suppressed by colonial powers. According to Mafundikwa, design has always been inherent to African culture and traditions.

Similarly, but on a larger scale, the International Indigenous Design Network (INDIGO) was formed in 2007 by the International Council of Graphic Design Associations (ICOGRADA) and the National Design Centre in Melbourne, Australia. This network promotes indigenous design as living culture, examines its relationship to national identity and its role as visual culture within contemporary society. The term indigenous in this context is broad and inclusive of every sort of visual expression that questions the notion of local design in a globalized world.

Activity: Socially responsible design

To promote the expansion of graphic design beyond conventional frames of reference, and to help maintain the international discourse of design and its role in sociocultural development, designers have to learn, promote, network and collaborate. Study the following recommendations on how to achieve socially responsible design and think about how you can introduce them into your design practice.

01	Build experience around the needs of people living in different contexts.
02	Network with international organizations and corporations in order to demonstrate the value of design.
03	Participate in multidisciplinary initiatives in which designers play a critical role in the development of social entrepreneurship and innovation.
04	Work on publications, events, exhibitions and competitions for design that promote creative initiatives for development.
05	Advocate the power of graphic design in a cultural context by organizing workshops and seminars and by encouraging cross-cultural exchange.
06	Evaluate the quality of design education across the world and multiply social design curricula.
07	Learn from professional organizations that can provide expertise, knowledge, guidance, contacts and ensure an international perspective and representation of design.
08	Create open information sources on design methodologies in partnership with public and private partners worldwide.
09	Provide new platforms where individuals and organizations can share best practices on a global scale.

Collaboration	Vision
	Technical
Consumption	Vision
	Technical
Efficiency	Vision
Entrepreneurship	
	Technical
Fair Trade	Vision
	Technical
Innovation	Vision
	Technical
Materials	Vision
New markets	
	Technical
Problem solving	Vision
Production	
	Technical
Reuse/Recycling	Vision
	Technical
Storytelling	Vision
Strategy	Vision
Technology	
	Technical

6.1 Technical and vision targets

The touch points from chapter 1 are shown here highlighting their most obvious applicability to technical or vision targets. In some cases, a particular target may be pertinent to both, depending on the context and nature of the organization.

Implementing Sustainable Practices

Implementing sustainable business practices requires some know-how and the ability to foresee how strategy can be applied in real world situations. Vision can be turned into actionable goals through the acquisition of relevant information and by creating a detailed plan.

This chapter presents frameworks and methodologies for adopting sustainable practices. It gives step-by-step guidelines for how to approach clients and members of one's own organization. The information provided is immediately applicable to professionals but can also be used by students as an example of how management skills can be applied in situations where social and environmental concerns are affecting business objectives.

Connecting sustainability and design management

How well ethically based design mandates are realized depends not only on vision, but also on effective communications skills, the use of a clearly articulated design process, and the organizational skills of managers and creative directors. As explored elsewhere in this text, including environmental and social objectives as part of management strategy can help to drive innovation and lead to the creation of new products and services. Subsequently, companies that are able to connect business strategy with sustainable development are able to hire designers who specialize in producing earth-friendly and human-centred outputs.

Making the transition to professional practice

Whether or not one makes social and environmental causes the centrepiece of professional practice, it is prudent to evaluate what role these issues have in one's life and whether they may affect career choices and the relationship one has with clients and co-workers. Such an examination can be used to aid in making informed work-related decisions and can also help young designers to begin to chart a career path.

It is useful to begin by asking the following questions (each of which is explored more fully in subsequent text): what are your ethical beliefs? Who do you want to work for? What are your skills? And, what are the social and environmental impacts of what you produce? Noting responses to these questions is a good way to begin exploring the relationship between social and environmental awareness and professional practice. Create a diagram of your answers and rate them in order of importance. Consider job opportunities available in your community or in your target location. Then, map out the steps you will need to take to attain a preferable employment situation, while still adhering to your personal and professional values.

6.2 Sustainability report

The NewPage paper sustainability report designed by Kuhlmann Leavitt, Inc., uses imagery to connect the company's products to the values it places on employees and manufacturing processes.

What are your ethical beliefs?

Understanding personal ideology and exploring the ethical ramifications associated with a given course of study are a necessary part of the education of a designer. Before beginning a career, it is helpful to identify the ideas and values that are most important to you professionally and personally. This information can be used as a guide when looking for employment and/or when developing a freelance practice.

Even in situations where a client or the particulars of a job do not allow a designer to make environmentally and socially conscious outputs, it is still possible to engage with the ethical dilemmas surrounding the work one makes. Taking part in discussions with clients and co-workers can help others to develop their own positions and may eventually have an impact on what is produced by a company or a client. As indicated in Chapter 4, there are also numerous opportunities for designers to connect with individuals who share their interests. Online resources and those associated with professional organizations can provide an outlet for creative individuals who are unable to produce sustainably driven work at their current job.

Who do you want to work for?

It can be difficult for new designers to make determinations about where they should seek employment. Personal values and ethical beliefs can be one important indicator when deciding what type of company one wants to work for. Another variable is workplace environment. For instance, working in a small studio will be very different from working at an agency or as an in-house designer at a large company.

Different people are suited to different situations so it is useful to learn as much about each setting as possible. Internships are a great way of finding out what it is like to work in a particular type of job. If ethical considerations are important to you, consider trying to find an internship at a non-profit organization or a company that makes environmentally or socially conscious products. If you cannot find listings suited to your interests, try putting an advert on an online job board. You can offer to work part-time as an intern if a company's values match your own. You might be surprised at how many sustainably minded companies are unable to hire full-time designers and would be delighted to have some part-time help.

What are your skills?

Regardless of what stage you are at in your career, it is important to understand your strengths. Students can use this information to decide what type of positions to apply for and professionals can evaluate whether their current job effectively utilizes their skills. Some individuals are naturally suited to organizational tasks or to presenting design work to clients. If this is the case, you might consider looking for a job where there will be opportunities to learn about design management. There are those people who are better at coming up with ideas, whereas others will excel at executing an existing vision. These variables all have an impact on the type of position that will be most suited to a particular individual.

Starting out

At the beginning of one's career, it can be difficult to conduct an accurate self-assessment. Students and young professionals should look to educators, mentors and even classmates for help. Many professional societies offer students the opportunity to have portfolio reviews with established designers. These reviews can be a good place to find out what an impartial individual thinks of your work. College professors, tutors and class-mates are also a good source of feedback. To elicit the best response, make sure to setup a meeting to discuss these issues face-to-face.

Evaluation

Even after one finishes school, it is important to re-evaluate your strengths and to consider your employment preferences. Semi-annual or annual evaluations by employers may provide some of this information, but ongoing self-assessment and external feedback are also needed. Review your portfolio and ask yourself which projects turned out the best and which you enjoyed working on the most. Examine why certain projects are more rewarding. When you can identify instances where one project (or more) is both successful and enjoyable, you may have found a type of work or area of specialization that is right for you.

Colleagues can also be a good source of information. Ask a fellow designer to rate which pieces in your portfolio they think are the best and why. Combine the feedback from others with your own preferences and create a profile of an 'ideal job'. Then assess your current position and try to figure out what you would need to do to attain a more preferable position (students should use assessment information to define their 'ideal job'). Work in incremental steps to obtain a preferable employment situation and do not be afraid to realign along the way.

What are the environmental and social impacts of your outputs?

As detailed elsewhere in this text, man-made materials and even some of the processes used to turn natural materials into usable goods can have a variety of negative impacts on the environment. Ask yourself how the materials you use in day-to-day design practice affect the environment throughout their life cycle. Do less harmful materials exist? Can some of the environmental effects of the production processes be mitigated?

In some instances, a communication designer may be able to work with an eco-friendly printer and specify FSC certified paper. Similarly, a product designer might be able to use natural or less harmful materials and when that is not feasible, it may be possible to use a material more efficiently or to design an object for easy deconstruction or recycling.

Even if you are unable to use environmentally preferable materials or production processes for every project, it is still useful to analyse what could be done in an ideal situation. In your portfolio, you can present eco-friendly or socially conscious alternatives along with examples of how the piece was actually produced. This is a great way for students to show that they care about particular issues and have the ability to think beyond the brief. It is also a useful technique for professionals who plan to seek new employment opportunities, or to advance in their current company or work situation.

Activity: Personal and professional values

By making notes on your responses to the following questions you can begin to identify where professional skills intersect with personal interests.

01	What are my ethical beliefs?
02	Who do I want to work for?
03	What are my skills?
04	What are the social consequences of what I produce?
05	What are the environmental impacts of what I produce?

6.3 The design process

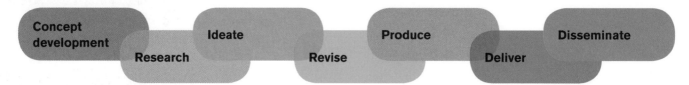

Concept development — Research — Ideate — Revise — Produce — Deliver — Disseminate

6.3 The design process
This graphic illustrates the main stages in the design process.

A note to designers

The information included in this section is scalable depending on the size of the organization and scope of a client's mandate. There are numerous opportunities to help companies retool their design, procurement and production practices, and create new ethically minded guidelines and procedures.

The design process

It is necessary to fully understand the mission of a company, its organizational structure, and the means it employs to produce market ready outputs before beginning to create an action plan for future improvement. Diagrams of the design process or a company's workflow can be used to examine how sustainable practices will affect various aspects of a company and interface with existing competencies or initiatives.

For some designers, a diagram may make it easier to see opportunities for improvement or specific areas that can be targeted. Non-designers also respond well to visual explanations. In some instances, an entire team can participate in brainstorming or mapping exercises, while in other situations, the designers on an integrated team may be given the role of visual interpreter. In these instances, diagrams and charts can facilitate understanding of current market positioning, how outputs are produced, and the ways in which current practices may be altered or revised. Visuals can be used either prior to or during the planning process. They may also be included in presentations to upper management or to potential clients and other stakeholders.

Working with social responsibility

Some companies create harmful products and are so out of alignment with one's values that many designers may decide not to take on such work. If in doubt, check the ethical guidelines from professional design organizations and/or join The Designers Accord. The Designers Accord offers guidelines on how to work ethically and is an opportunity to become part of a like-minded community.

Strategy

Implementing sustainable business practices and publicly identifying as an ethically driven company can provide opportunities to connect existing strategy with new objectives. Socially and environmentally conscious outputs should complement current strategy and long-term goals. When the two are incompatible, it is less likely that a proposal or plan will receive support from fellow employees and senior management. If institutional objectives seem to be at odds with the goals of the sustainability working group, it might be necessary to think more broadly about whether the mission of the company fully reflects its values and/or to create a plan that targets one area at a time, and that can be implemented in distinct phases over several years.

Creating a system

By analysing current practices, evaluating future goals, and investigating the nature and mission of an organization, it is possible to create a customized structure and set of goals that will act as a guide for changing business practices. The following system can also be used as a tool when starting a company. It was developed as a way for designers and clients in a variety of industries to shift their workflow and make lasting improvements.

Designer first

A wealth of information is available dealing with the relevant theories associated with sustainability. Designers should research the materials and processes associated with socially and environmentally responsible design before approaching clients to offer new eco-friendly options. New designers may apply knowledge learned during their studies and are sometimes hired specifically for that expertise, whereas more established professionals often use the skill attained for one job to apply to their next endeavour. Duke Stump's work as a consultant is directly informed by his experience of working at Nike and Seventh Generation, and Leonora Oppenheim's experience of working for TreeHugger gave her a solid foundation of relevant practical information to draw upon when she started Elio Studio.

Steps to creating sustainable practices

- Form a working group.

- Research and analyse.

- Review the company's mission, who you are, and what you do.

- Identify ways sustainability can fit into the culture of the company.

- Create vision and technical targets.

- Set a timeline for implementation.

- Create measurable benchmarks for evaluation and ways to assess how successful the initiative has been.

- Internally market and communicate information about the new strategy.

- Implement the strategy.

- Evaluate and assess based on timeline, milestones and goals.

- Make revisions if needed.

Client first

When a client asks the designer for ways to be more eco-friendly, the process of identifying solutions and goals can be rewarding for both parties. The client and designer can embark on a fact-finding mission together. A client may assign an internal team to work with the designer to identify areas of improvement, or an individual designer or firm may work as a consultant and propose changes. In the latter case, the client and consultant will often engage in a series of dialogues with the designer to decide what changes are cost effective, easiest to accomplish and most acutely needed.

Depending on the size and requirements of a job, there may be additional costs associated with eco-friendly production or fabrication. It is important to be clear about the costs and benefits associated with speccing new or environmentally preferable materials and production. It may also be necessary to remind the client or company that being a sustainable company may not immediately help improve the financial bottom line, but it can have other benefits that align with a company's mission and improve a brand's image.

Beating price premiums

The cost of environmentally preferable materials is trending downward. In some cases, it might be necessary to research new materials or vendors that offer environmentally preferable services that do not add to the overall costs of a job. Additionally, if greater efficiency can be achieved or a longer lifespan for a product is possible, these factors may mitigate any cost difference for the client and consumer.

Quick steps for designers

Below are three ways designers can improve their own practice and positively effect change.

Improve efficiency

This is an area that is often overlooked; but can bring about some of the most immediate and cost effective change. It may require analysis of existing systems, quantities produced, and ways of disseminating information.

Target materials and production

Most people think of this when they consider sustainable design. It can include specifying environmentally preferable materials and manufacturing, and working with new technology. At times, it may even require a designer to change vendors to take advantage of new options, such as switching to digital outputs, or working with eco-friendly raw materials or non-hardware based assembly of products.

Utilize design thinking and problem solving

In the long run, the power of sustainable design is going to be more about thinking and problem solving than it is about materials and production. Design is not just about visual styling, it is also about analysis and ideas, so remember to bill clients for that time as well. Partnering with designers from other disciplines offers opportunities to be a catalyst for change in a variety of design-related areas.

Buy-in

It is absolutely vital that the participants and employees who are going to be asked to shift their jobs, or take on new responsibilities, have the opportunity to give input. While it may not be appropriate to invite every employee to participate, it should be possible to choose one person from each functional group (i.e. interface design, art direction, and production management) to take part in a sustainability working group or workshop. These employees can report back to others. Managers may take part in or oversee the working group directly, or they can allow these employees to function semi-autonomously and simply require regular progress updates. In small companies or studios this may mean that one or two people work on sustainability initiatives for as little as a few hours a week.

Support from the top

It is laudable for employees at every level in a company to look for ways to achieve greater efficiency and identify more environmentally friendly working processes. However, if one wants to implement an organization-wide set of policies or directives, it is absolutely essential there is clear support and buy-in from top management. It may be unrealistic for upper management to be involved in a specific task force or working group, but a message of endorsement and/or a brief appearance can go a long way toward making employees feel that their work is valued, and the goals that are identified as part of the working process will also be supported by senior management.

6.4 HÄG Capisco Puls
Scandinavian Business Seating is an example of a company that is using sustainable products and environmentally friendly materials when creating their range of office seating.

169

Identify a working group

When implementing sustainable practices within an organization or company, the first thing that will need to be done is to decide who will be involved. One can begin by identifying a list of participants (including students) who will be part of a core working group and can evangelize, cheer and lead the call for change. It is more important that the participants have the time, have an interest in helping to implement change and represent the different areas in the organization that will be affected by the new system, than have existing expertise.

Students working together in a group setting may decide to produce a socially or environmentally conscious output, even if the project does not stipulate such criteria. In these instances, one or more students may take the lead and conduct research and visual explorations that pertain to the project content.

Setting aside time

Students and freelance designers may have free time to devote to learning about sustainable practices including new materials, production methods and certifications. However, in a busy workplace, it is often hard to carve out time for small projects let alone be part of a new working group. It is essential all participants in job-specific groups be given ample time (even if this includes exemptions from other duties) to do the research and to achieve the targets and goals that have been identified. Additionally, participants should be given time to attend meetings and workshops.

Students often get into workshops, conferences and lectures for free or at a lower cost than professionals do. Taking part in this type of activity as a student is a great way to broaden one's knowledge base and make connections with like-minded people.

Choosing a facilitator/s

Choose one or two members of the team who can facilitate the group and run meetings. This person(s) can come from management or be someone with some expertise in sustainability or environmental performance.

It is equally important to define roles when working on group projects as a student. Evaluate each person's skill level and knowledge base. Choosing one student to facilitate meetings and keep track of the timeline is a good way to begin developing management skills. When working on student projects participants may take turns to lead the project, so several people are able to gain experience in project management.

Research and analysis

The working group should begin by analysing the type of work/outputs produced by the company and identifying ways that sustainability can dovetail with the company's mission and existing goals and objectives.

Depending on the degree to which production and materials usage are part of a company's output, research will need to be conducted to find preferable materials, new vendors and improved production or manufacturing methods.

The group should identify areas that can be targeted when trying to achieve sustainable practices. This should include a list of ways that consumers, employees and stakeholders will be affected by new mandates or policies.

6.5 Working together

NODE is a non-profit social business group working to combine great design with fair trade projects. NODE invited French illustrator Chamo to design this rug and collaborate with a Nepalese fair trade group as part of a collection for The Design Museum shop in London (UK).

Activity: Setting up a working group	**Practitioners**	
	01	Set aside a morning for the working group to identify which areas of the company or organization's mission can be connected to social and environmental responsibility.
	02	Research what other comparable organizations are doing, and create a short report or bulleted list (see benchmarking, page 50).
	03	Make a list of ways the company's mission or mandate dovetails with sustainability.

	Students	
	01	Identify a non-profit group or a local/regional business whose mission can be connected to social and environmental responsibility.
	02	Research what this group does or produces and who they serve (if a for-profit business, who are their consumers?). Are competitors (or similar organizations) adopting more earth-friendly or humane practices? If so, are they successful? If not, why not?
	03	Make a list of ways the company's mission or mandate dovetails with sustainability.

6.6

Marketing and communication

How much time is spent on marketing and the dissemination of new practices will depend on the size of the company and/or whether or not it is a new business. In the case of a small company, marketing new practices may not be appropriate, and dissemination may be as easy as briefing co-workers during meetings and talking to vendors individually. The larger the organization, the more important it will be to get the word out that the working group has come up with a set of targets and action points that are going to affect various groups within the company. Some of this information may even be appropriate to include in an annual report or message to stakeholders and consumers. For example, large organizations such as the United Nations have thousands of employees who work in countries all over the world. To disseminate the implementation of sustainable practices, the UN created an online resource (see www.greeningtheblue.org) that would serve as receptacle for information targeted to employees of the UN and the general public. Check the website to see how this was achieved.

Students and freelance designers can incorporate information about their interest and experience of sustainable design on their personal website or as part of a portfolio. Highlighting the ways in which a student project took social and environmental issues into account can be a good way of marketing one's skills. Clients, potential employers and reviewers for graduate school or PhD programmes often look for attributes that differentiate candidates and/or show a unique aspect of their work or ideas. Consider emphasizing issues of personal importance, while also showcasing your strongest design work.

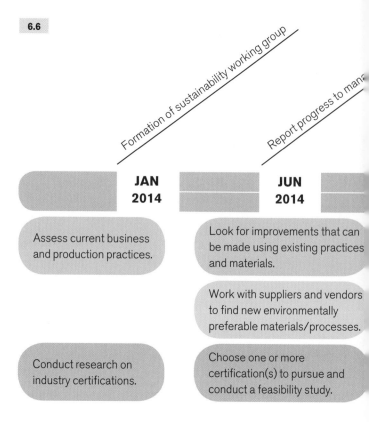

Formation of sustainability working group

Report progress to man[...]

JAN 2014

JUN 2014

Assess current business and production practices.

Look for improvements that can be made using existing practices and materials.

Work with suppliers and vendors to find new environmentally preferable materials/processes.

Conduct research on industry certifications.

Choose one or more certification(s) to pursue and conduct a feasibility study.

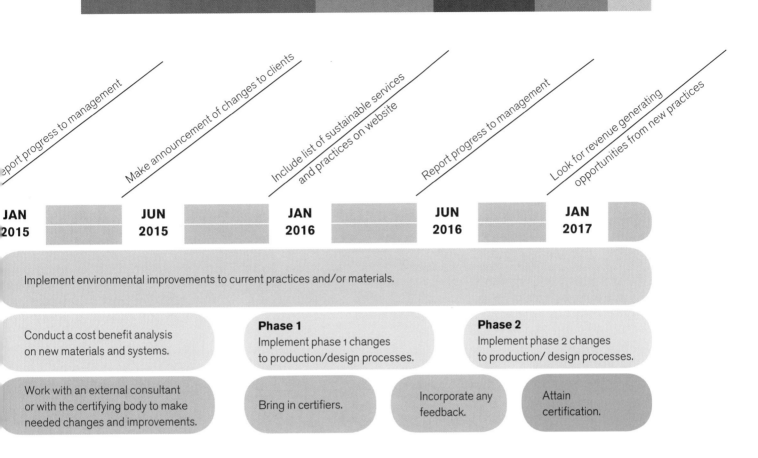

Report progress to management

Make announcement of changes to clients

Include list of sustainable services and practices on website

Report progress to management

Look for revenue generating opportunities from new practices

| JAN 2015 | JUN 2015 | JAN 2016 | JUN 2016 | JAN 2017 |

Implement environmental improvements to current practices and/or materials.

Conduct a cost benefit analysis on new materials and systems.

Phase 1
Implement phase 1 changes to production/design processes.

Phase 2
Implement phase 2 changes to production/ design processes.

Work with an external consultant or with the certifying body to make needed changes and improvements.

Bring in certifiers.

Incorporate any feedback.

Attain certification.

Financial resources

Consider whether additional financial resources will be necessary or if existing funds will need to be reallocated. Items that require funding may include incentive programmes, new equipment and investment in infrastructure, increased costs for technology, training or certifications. The working group should interface with management to ensure it has adequate resources to meet all targets and goals.

Targeting change

When creating actionable benchmarks for sustainable production and business practices, it is helpful to identify what type of targets one is trying to achieve. In many cases, an organization, solo designer or company will benefit from creating a strategy that includes vision targets as well as technical targets. However, in narrowly defined situations it might be most expedient to focus on only one of these areas.

6.6 Create a timeline

Create a working timeline for the implementation of the proposed changes. Planning for sustainable practice requires flexibility and one should always plan to revise goals and due dates when the need arises. Consider one-, three- and five-year timelines with milestones outlining what will be accomplished when.

Vision targets

Vision targets address the big picture and should be focused on how sustainability can fit into the mission and the intended outcomes of an organization. They should be seen as a long-range vision of an organization's goals and how they relate to social and environmental responsibility. Finally, they should complement the company's mission and purpose. Vision targets should be applicable to all employees and stakeholders.

If an organization does not have a stated mission or purpose that employees are familiar with, the working group can create one for the specific purpose of adopting sustainable values. For instance, during a 2008 Sustainable United Nations Publishing workshop at UN headquarters in New York City, participants found the UN's mission lacked the specifics they needed to develop applicable vision targets. The group came up with a division-specific mission that referred to a 'code of ethics', which was an internal term for 'vision targets'. (For more information see www.un.org.)

6.7 Alternative vision targets
Vision targets will vary depending on the context and the specifics of an organization.

6.7 | ## Examples of vision targets

To develop a design practice that maintains the highest level of social and environmental standards.

To explore how industry-based certifications and information sharing networks can help improve environmental performance and creative output to make the office environment as healthy and waste free as possible.

To create new design outputs or products that are based on their environmental performance.

To use design skills to improve the lives of the people who use our products.

To achieve increased profitability while still maintaining and/or improving best practices and environmental performance.

To develop a brand that puts social and environmental values at the forefront of its business practices and marketing.

To identify and use production practices and materials that are less harmful to the environment; to annually donate five per cent of employees' time to pro bono or community-based work.

Pros and cons of vision targets

When creating vision targets, it is important to begin with what is known. For instance, one can ask, 'Given the specific mission of the organization what should the overall environmental goals be?' It is then possible to make a list of goals and objectives that will become the targets for the overall vision of a company. It is essential to begin with the mission and core values of a company so the identified goals and benchmarks will work within the existing organizational structure.

- **Pros:** Easy to understand, provide overarching view, are widely applicable, take into account long-term goals.

- **Cons:** Not always immediately actionable, may be lacking in specifics, and may be seen as too conceptual by some participants.

Activity: Create a working draft

Practitioners

01	Set aside a morning for the working group to have a brainstorming session during which they create a working draft of vision targets.
02	Gather input on the working draft from managers and employees affected by targets. Keep in mind that in a big organization there are many people involved, so managing the various stakeholders may be a challenge.
03	Incorporate feedback and put targets into the timeline.
04	Share vision targets with employees and stakeholders outside the working group through internal marketing or information sessions.

Students

01	Working in small groups or as a class, conduct a brainstorming session using the list previously created outlining how the organization's mission or mandate dovetails with sustainability to identify specific areas for improvement. Then, develop one or more vision targets for each.
02	Create a proposed plan of action for the company or organization. It should include who would be affected by your proposals, as well as a timeline listing items that need to be accomplished.
03	Visually design the plan and create a diagram of the timeline. The overall appearance should be similar to a competition proposal.

Technical targets

Technical targets are much more concrete than vision targets. The specifics of technical targets vary widely depending on what an organization produces. They may address some or all of the following areas: materials, processes, technology, procurement, innovation, vendors and specifications. Technical targets are immediate and actionable. They may only be applicable to one group or division within a company, but they may also require company-wide policy changes.

For example, a campaign that required employees to recycle all materials used in an office would include technical targets that dealt with the need for new bins and a vendor to pick up and recycle the materials. In other cases, technical targets may require the purchase of new equipment and training or retraining of existing personnel.

If appropriate, technical targets can be adopted based on the guidelines from one or more certifying bodies (such as ISO, see pages 96–7), but they can also be customized to suit the needs of a specific organization. Technical targets should provide clearly actionable goals and policies for both the short and long term. They should include continual improvement and specify which groups, employees or vendors will be affected by recommended changes.

Targets need to be realistic. Of course, one wants perfection, but it should be achieved in incremental steps. Consider a multi-step, five-year plan; try to raise the bar, and look for ways to improve.

The working group that took part in the 2008 Sustainable United Nations Publishing workshop identified targets for sustainable operations in the following areas: materials/energy, people, process, technologies and policy. Additionally, they decided that attaining ISO 14000 certification for all UN Publishing operations would be one of the first goals the duty stations would work toward.

Several examples of possible technical targets identified during the 2008 Sustainable United Nations Publishing workshop included:

- Comprehensive management of all waste materials and energy utilization for each duty station. Materials will include paper, ink, plates, plastic, metals, chemicals, water, rubber, cloth and containers.

- Research/acquire/promote sustainable technologies (such as waterless printing, direct to press, digital and energy-efficient machinery).

- Influence procurement practices to be consistent with green publishing, including mandate to partner with environmentally conscious vendors.

Pros and cons of technical targets

- **Pros:** Specific, actionable directives.

- **Cons:** Highly technical, difficult to understand, can include too much information, and not applicable to every position/process.

Activity: Achieving technical targets

Practitioners

01	Set aside a morning for the working group to make a list of possible areas to focus the technical targets. Additional information may be needed from various areas of a company, so make a list of general categories that can be included in technical targets.
02	Conduct research on each of the proposed target areas and the group should reconvene at a later date to share and compare information.
03	Revise and fit the technical targets into a working draft.
04	Gather input from managers and other employees on the draft of targets.
05	Revise technical targets and put them into the timeline.
06	Share finished targets and timeline with employees and management.

Students

01	Make a list of the production process you used to produce one or more student projects (please note that different types of designers will use different processes).
02	Choose one of these processes (and its related materials) to concentrate on for this activity.
03	Evaluate the environmental ramifications associated with the materials and production techniques used. Use online research, information from manufacturers and other sources of secondary research to determine what the most harmful effects of these processes are.
04	Create a plan for how to mitigate negative environmental effects. Your plan may include using less material in the first place, purchasing preferable substances, changing production process, etc. Evaluate the biggest impediments to change (i.e. cost, time, availability) and create a timeline, which focuses on improvements that are the easiest to achieve first and then on more difficult ones. Your timeline can be as short as one year or as long as five years.

What works best

Working with a combination of vision and technical targets can provide a powerful tool to achieve long-term sustainable practices. Vision targets provide the big picture view and can complement existing business strategy, while technical targets give specific steps for organizations and their employees to follow. One must be realistic about what can be achieved in a given amount of time. Create one-, three- and five-year plan with targets for each. This system can apply to one's own company or when doing external work with clients. In either case, placing short- and long-range goals on a timeline can help to maintain focus.

SMART/ER project objectives

Creating objectives is important in many workplaces and creative situations. The acronym SMART/ER stands for a way of thinking about setting objectives and evaluating goals for a given project. The term is widely used in project and performance management, but using the SMART/ER system for defining and evaluating objectives and goals has applicability to a wide range of organizations.

SMART/ER objectives

- Specific
- Measurable
- Attainable
- Relevant
- Time-bound
- Evaluate
- Re-evaluate environmentally conscious vendors

One stop shopping

Consider creating a library or other collaborative tool for information that has been identified by the working group. This virtual and/or physical clearing house should be accessible to everyone in the organization. By doing so, new employees and those working in different divisions do not have to duplicate each other's work. The format for this new library of information may be digital or physical, but should allow data and information to be easily accessed across offices and among employees.

How you share the information you have found will vary depending on the size of the organization you work for and the type of design work that you produce. New York City-based design studio, Two Twelve, found that putting resources in binders and creating sustainability checklists worked best for their workflow. At Open House, a Tokyo-based product design company, samples of materials are on shelves, tables and generally all over the studio. Their system seems more haphazard to the casual viewer, but Open House only has a handful of employees and works exclusively on sustainable design, so there is less of a need to differentiate between eco-friendly and non-eco-friendly products. The single best reason to create your own materials/production library is because it saves time, so find a system that works best for you and start sharing information.

Digital libraries are more accessible and easier to manage, but in the case of materials-specific databases, such as those used for environmental design, product design, or even papers for graphic designers, having a library of physical samples may be necessary for final specification.

6.8

6.9

6.8–6.9 Fair trade goods
Goods marked with Fairtrade labels
provide assurance about how products are
produced. Here Fairtrade cotton is being
picked for products destined for the British
retailer Marks & Spencer.

Activity: Share resources	Practitioners	
	01	Research new materials and processes.
	02	Create an information clearing house/library to store materials and information.
	03	Let others know the resource exists and how to access it.

	Students	
	01	Work as a group to create a classroom resource for issues, materials or processes related to sustainable design. For instance, students of product design may find a 'library' of new materials most useful where as multi-disciplinary designers may want to gather relevant theoretical writings or collect examples of the ways in which different professional designers have applied fair trade practices to their work.
	02	Using research databases (such as LexisNexis, ProQuest or ScienceDirect), websites and books, gather information about the topic.
	03	Create an information clearing house/library to store materials and information. Consider using large ring binders with some sort of indexing system, or make the information available online via links.
	04	Make the information available to other students by putting the binders/hard copies of information in an accessible place or by inviting others to use the online resource.

Conclusion

A range of different perspectives, business objectives and personal beliefs can affect professional design practice. Given the complexity of the problems designers are asked to solve, it is useful to explore how different approaches to content/object creation, visual styling, and communication can impact the overall success of designed products and services. Understanding these variables is imperative for students looking to work professionally.

The preceding chapters highlighted a variety of organizational and management tools that are applicable to the creative process. The principles described in this book are customizable and can be applied to a wide range of design and business applications. A thorough understanding of these methodologies and competencies will enable designers and students to engage with an audience and create more effective design deliverables.

Moving forward

As eco-friendly and efficient as one can make production and technical processes, projects still begin with a client, a designer, and content or product creation. You have a greater chance of success if you begin the process of moving toward sustainable solutions before being faced with a specific job. The methods and tools discussed in this book aim to provide readers with an understanding of the core elements of design management and how those can be used in combination with sustainable thinking to produce client-ready outputs.

By showcasing examples of best practice and providing resources for implementation in real time this book seeks to enable employees, managers, and stakeholders to more easily imagine making a shift towards more sustainable practices themselves.

Early adopters and organizations that are in a leadership position have an obligation to share knowledge and to encourage innovation and best practices by working with like-minded companies or vendors. As stated elsewhere in this text, it is often a combination of exterior pressures and interior culture that creates the impetus for change within an organization. Recent graduates are in an ideal position to pass on information about sustainable thinking to employers and fellow-employees. A combination of shared knowledge and internal and external pressures is most likely to produce the sea change needed to fundamentally improve the environmental and social performance of design deliverables and products.

Making a declaration

A carefully worded declaration can increase buy-in among low- and mid-level employees and, by virtue of the fact that management is required to sign it, a declaration can also provide a reminder that those in charge support a set of principles and goals. Having that piece of paper with executive signatures and ratification is like an insurance policy, an advertisement, and an incentive device all rolled into one. A declaration can help to ensure that policies are enacted and that employees and stakeholders will go the distance to implement goals and objectives that have been identified by the working group.

Whether or not this is a useful or effective tool is up to you, but consider that The Designers Accord is basically a declaration and over 100,000 designers have signed it. Also imagine if every graduating design student signed a declaration to uphold a set of social and environmental principles. Even if only half followed through on their promise, the world would be a much better place.

For the foreseeable future, issues associated with the production and distribution of design deliverables will continue to challenge design practitioners. Incremental changes have a cumulative effect and when problems are broken down into individual steps and supported by appropriate goals and objectives they are rarely insurmountable. The central aim of this book has been to examine how effective strategy and creative problem solving can be combined with a sensitivity toward environmental and social issues to produce designers who are capable of using 'sustainable thinking' to approach problems large and small.

Outreach

- Make what you know and what you have learned available to others whenever possible.

- Educate stakeholders, consumers and end users so they value sustainable processes and products.

- Help to create and steer a market for sustainable goods and services.

- Work with like-minded vendors and companies whenever possible.

Glossary

Backcasting

Backcasting is strategic tool used in sustainable development. One starts by defining a point in the future (that will include more desirable/ sustainable living standards) or by envisioning a desirable prospect and then works backwards to identify the programmes, policies and changes that will need to happen in order to connect the present to future.

Biodynamic agriculture

Nature's forces are used to achieve a balance in the interrelationships of land, plants, and animals so a self-nourishing system is created that does not need chemical fertilizers or other external inputs. Originating with the work of Rudolf Steiner, an Austrian-born philosopher and social thinker, biodynamic agriculture was one of the first ecological farming systems and focuses on observation of natural systems and using that information to disturb the land and cycle of life as little as possible.

Carbon footprint

The sum of all emissions and greenhouse gasses, like CO_2, that are produced by a person's activities, the goods they buy, and services they use within a given timeframe.

Certification

Independent third-party certifiers evaluate a given industry, production process, or the sourcing of a raw material to ensure that it adheres to a specific set to criteria. Certifiers make information about how materials and production processes are evaluated available to the public. These organizations often encourage the use of a mark or visual symbol to show that a product has met the relevant standards.

Closed-loop system

An ecological system that does not rely on inputs from, or matter to be exchanged from, outside of the system. Some or all outputs of the system are also used as inputs.

Cottage industry

A small-scale industry where products or services are usually produced at home or by family members using their own equipment rather than in a factory.

Cradle-to-cradle principles

In *Cradle to Cradle: Remaking the Way We Make Things* (North Point Press, 2002), William McDonough and Michael Braungart proposed that products should be designed so that after their useful lives are over they can provide 'nourishment' for something new. Cradle-to-cradle principles are guided by the notion that, in the natural world, waste equals food. McDonough and Braungart suggest that currently we 'downcycle' rather that recycle. With each subsequent use, we produce lower grade material until we are finally left with unusable waste that can only be incinerated or stored in landfills. McDonough and Braungart say that we are in need of an industrial re-evolution in which we will eliminate the concept of waste and instead design products and systems that can provide nourishment for something new at the end of their useful lives.

Externalities

An externality is an unintended consequence of an economic activity where one party, who is not involved in a transaction, is affected by the transaction, product or service. Externalities can be positive or negative; they may occur during any phase of a product's life cycle. Externalities may affect both the consumer and the producer and, when negative, they are an excellent example of the failure to solve an overall design problem.

Fair trade

A market-based approach that seeks to help producers and workers in developing countries attain fair wages and equitable working conditions. In most cases this means that consumers in wealthy countries pay a higher price for a commodity or product because there is some assurance or regulation that producers have received better wages and work in better social and environmental conditions. Fair trade organizations abide by different guidelines so it is important to understand there is no universally accepted set of standards. Each organization will have their own criteria and may offer a certification based on supply chain assessments.

First Things First

A manifesto first presented in 1964 and again in 2000 in which signatories in the visual arts agreed to use their work for the advancement of social justice everywhere.

NGO (non-governmental organization)

A legally constituted organization that operates independently from any government and often pursues a social or environmentally sensitive mission.

Product life cycle

The stages a product goes through from the time of its manufacture to its recycling or disposal.

Social entrepreneurs

People who recognize a problem or challenge and use entrepreneurship principles or other innovative solutions to create and manage a business or other undertaking with the goal of making positive social change.

Supply chain

A system that organizes people, resources, technology, production, and distribution so there is a way to track a product from its beginnings as raw materials to eventual use and disposal.

Sustainable

Forms of human economic activity and culture that do not lead to environmental degradation, especially avoiding the long-term depletion of natural resources. The *Oxford English Dictionary* also includes a definition relating to development: 'Utilization and development of natural resources in ways that are compatible with the maintenance of these resources, and with the conservation of the environment, for future generations'.

Triple-bottom line

Refers to a balanced exchange of goods and services (beyond just profit) that takes into account the social, environmental, and economic and implications of way of an organizations' output and performance.

Victor Papanek

Beginning in the 1970s with his publication *Design for the Real World: Human Ecology and Social Change (Thames & Hudson, 1985)*, Papanek, an industrial designer, suggested a renewed focus on the end user and believed that designers had an obligation to work for the greater good and not just the financial well-being of their clients. He railed against built-in obsolescence and his ideas are widely credited with injecting ethics, accountability, and environmental sensitivity into the design-making process.

Bibliography

Aldersey-Williams, Hugh, et al. *Design and the Elastic Mind.* New York: The Museum of Modern Art, 2008.

Andraos, Amale and Wood, Dan. *Above the Pavement – the Farm! Architecture & Agriculture at PF1.* New York: Princeton Architectural Press, 2010.

Bell, Bryan, Wakeford, Katie, et al. *Expanding Architecture: Design as Activism.* New York: Metropolis Books, 2008.

Benyus, Janine M. *Biomimicry: Innovation Inspired by Nature.* New York: Harper Perennial, 2002.

Berger, Warren. *Glimmer: How Design Can Transform Your Life, and Maybe Even the World.* New York: Penguin Press, 2009.

Berman, David B. *Do Good Design: How Designers Can Change the World.* Berkeley, CA: Peachpit Press, 2008.

Best, Kathryn. *Design Management: Managing Design Strategy, Process and Implementation.* London: AVA Academia, 2006.

Best, Kathryn. *The Fundamentals of Design Management.* London: AVA Academia, 2010.

Birkeland, Janis. *Design for Sustainability: A Sourcebook of Integrated, Eco-logical Solutions.* London: Earthscan Publications Ltd, 2002.

Borja De Mozota, Brigitte. *Design Management.* New York: Allworth Press, 2003.

Boylston, Scott. *Designing Sustainable Packaging.* London: Laurence King Publishing, 2009.

Braungart, Michael and McDonough, William. *Cradle to Cradle: Remaking the Way We Make Things.* New York: North Point Press, 2002.

Brown, Tim. *Change By Design: How Design Thinking Transforms Organizations and Inspires Innovation.* New York: HarperBusiness, 2009.

Busch, Akiko. *The Uncommon Life of Common Objects.* New York: Metropolis Books, 2005.

Chapman, Jonathan and Gant, Nick. *Designers, Visionaries and Other Stories: A Collection of Sustainable Design Essays.* London: Earthscan Publications Ltd, 2007.

Chick, Anne, and Micklethwaite, Paul. *Design for Sustainable Change: How Design and Designers Can Drive the Sustainability Agenda.* London: AVA Academia, 2011.

Cleveland, Jonathan and Top, Peleg. *Designing for the Greater Good: The Best in Cause-Related Marketing and Nonprofit Design.* New York: Harper Design, 2010.

Dean, Andrea Oppenheimer and Hursley, Timothy. *Rural Studio: Samuel Mockbee and an Architecture of Decency.* New York: Princeton Architectural Press, 2002.

DesJardins, Joseph R. *Environmental Ethics: An Introduction to Environmental Philosophy.* 4th ed. Belmont: Thompson Wadsworth, 2006.

Dougherty, Brian. *Green Graphic Design.* New York: Allworth Press, 2008.

Edwards, Andres R. *The Sustainability Revolution: Portrait of a Paradigm Shift.* Gabriola Island, BC: New Society Publishers, 2005.

Ehrenfeld, John R. *Sustainability by Design: A Subversive Strategy for Transforming Our Consumer Culture.* New Haven: Yale University Press, 2009.

Frascara, J., Kalsi, A. and Kneebone, P. *Graphic Design for Development.* Paris: Crea No 39, 1987, UNESCO Division of Cultural Development and Artistic Creation.

Fry, Tony. *Design Futuring: Sustainability, Ethics and New Practice.* Oxford: Berg Publishers, 2008.

Fuad-Luke, Alastair. *Design Activism: Beautiful Strategies for a Sustainable World.* New York: Routledge, 2009.

Fuad-Luke, Alastair. *EcoDesign: The Sourcebook.* San Francisco: Chronicle Books, 2006.

Giudice, Fabio, La Rosa, Guido and Risitano, Antonino. *Product Design for the Environment: A Life Cycle Approach.* Boca Raton, FL: CRC Press, 2006.

Hawken, Paul, Lovins, Amory and Lovins, Hunter L. *Natural Capitalism: Creating the Next Industrial Revolution.* New York: Back Bay Books, 2008.

Holston, David. *The Strategic Designer: Tools and Techniques for Managing the Design Process.* Cincinnati, Ohio: How Books, 2011.

Honda, Masahiro (preface). *Earth-Friendly Graphics.* Tokyo: PIE Books, 2006.

Imhoff, Daniel. *Paper Or Plastic: Searching for Solutions to an Overpackaged World.* Sierra Club Books, 2005.

Jedlicka, Wendy. *Packaging Sustainability: Tools, Systems and Strategies for Innovative Package Design.* New York: John Wiley & Sons, 2008.

Jedlicka, Wendy. *Sustainable Graphic Design: Tools, Systems and Strategies for Innovative Print Design.* New York: John Wiley & Sons, 2009.

John Chris Jones. *Design Methods.* New York: John Wiley & Sons, 1970.

Jones, Ellis. *The Better World Shopping Guide – 2nd Edition: Every Dollar Makes a Difference. Vol. 184.* Gabriola Island, BC: New Society Publishers, 2008.

Laszlo, Chris. *Sustainable Value: How the World's Leading Companies are Doing Well by Doing Good.* Stanford: Stanford Business Books, 2008.

Lockwood, Thomas. *Building Design Strategy: Using Design to Achieve Key Business Objectives.* New York: Allworth Press, 2008.

Lockwood, Thomas. *Design Thinking: Integrating Innovation, Customer Experience and Brand Value.* New York: Allworth Press, 2009.

Mallory, Rachel and Ohlman, Zachary. *Experimental EcoDesign: Product, Architecture, Fashion.* London: RotoVision, 2005.

Mau, Bruce. *Massive Change.* London: Phaidon Press, 2004.

McLennan, Jason F. *The Philosophy of Sustainable Design.* Bainbridge Island, WA: Ecotone Publishing, 2006.

Papanek, Victor. *Design for the Real World: Human Ecology and Social Change.* Chicago: Academy Chicago Publishers, 2005.

Papanek, Victor. *The Green Imperative: Ecology and Ethics in Design and Architecture.* London: Thames & Hudson, 1995.

Pfrunder, Manuela. *Neotopia.* Zurich: Limmat Verlag, 2002.

Pilloton, Emily. *Design Revolution: 100 Products That Are Changing People's Lives.* New York: Metropolis Books, 2009.

Poole, Buzz (editor). *Green Design.* New York: Mark Batty Publisher, 2007.

Proctor, Rebecca. *1000 New Eco Designs and Where to Find Them.* London: Laurence King Publishing, 2009.

Roberts, Lucienne. *Good: An introduction to Ethics in Graphic Design.* Lausanne: AVA Publishing, 2006.

Rogers, Heather. *Gone Tomorrow: The Hidden Life of Garbage.* New York: The New Press, 2005.

Ryan, Eric and Lowry, Adam. *The Method Method.* New York: Portfolio Penguin, 2009.

Shedroff, Nathan. *Design is the Problem: The Future of Design Must be Sustainable.* New York: Rosenfeld Media, 2009.

Sherin, Aaris. *SustainAble: A Handbook of Materials and Applications for Graphic Designers and their Clients.* Beverly, MA: Rockport Publishers, 2008.

Simmons, Christopher. *Just Design: Socially Conscious Design for Critical Causes.* Cincinnati, Ohio: How Books, 2011.

Smith, Cynthia E. *Design for the Other 90%.* New York: Cooper-Hewitt Museum, 2007.

Soyka, Peter A. *Creating a Sustainable Organization: Approaches for Enhancing Corporate Value Through Sustainability.* Upper Saddle River, New Jersey: FT Press, 2012.

Steffen, Alex. *Worldchanging: A User's Guide for the 21st Century.* New York: Abrams, 2008.

Stone, Terry Lee. *Managing the Design Process: Concept Development.* Beverly, MA: Rockport Publishers, 2010.

Stone, Terry Lee. *Managing the Design Process: Implementing Design.* Beverly, MA: Rockport Publishers, 2010.

Vezzoli, Carlo Arnaldo and Manzini, Ezio. *Design for Environmental Sustainability.* New York: Springer, 2010.

Walker, Brian Harrison and David Salt. *Resilience Thinking: Sustaining Ecosystems and People in a Changing World.* Washington DC: Island Press, 2006.

Walker, Stuart. *Sustainable by Design: Explorations in Theory and Practice.* Washington DC: Earthscan Publications Ltd, 2006.

Walker, Stuart. *The Spirit of Design: Objects, Environment and Meaning.* Washington DC: Earthscan Publications Ltd, 2001.

Werbach, Adam. *Strategy for Sustainability: A Business Manifesto.* Boston, MA: Harvard Business School Press, 2009.

Online resources

bigpicture.tv
Bigpicture TV is a UK-based online video information resource focused on the business impact of key environmental and social issues. Videos include content on resource management, manufacturing, energy resources, water use, product design, waste, philanthropy, and overseas development.

conservatree.com
Conserve a Tree seeks to be a one-stop source for information on environmental papers. It includes information on the environmental ramifications of the paper industry and advice for both large and small-scale purchasers.

designbynature.org
Design By Nature is an Australian site that offers general information on sustainability for graphic designers including info on paper, forestry, printing, a sample print spec sheet, as well as a case studies section on the work of environmentally conscious Australian designers. Design By Nature has some of the most extensive information on eco-friendly printing available.

designcanchange.org
Design Can Change is a Canadian resource and networking site that helps designers who want to work together to combat climate change.

designersaccord.org
The Designers Accord is a global coalition of designers, educators, and business leaders working together to create positive environmental and social impact. Adopters of the Designers Accord commit to five guidelines that provide ways to take action.

designigniteschange.org
Design Ignites Change: Engages students in multidisciplinary design and architecture projects that address pressing social issues.

design21sdn.com
Design 21: Social Design Network seeks to inspire social activism through design. The site connects people who want to explore the ways that design can positively impact on the worlds and who want to create change.

element21.ch
Element 21: Network of designers committed to solving local and international problems through innovative and creative solutions.

environmentalpaper.org
Environmental Paper Network: This site is graphic design specific, but it offers a lot of information about environmentally preferable paper options, and it is hosted by environmental organizations.

good.is
GOOD is a media platform including a magazine, website and video content that promotes, connects, and reports on the individuals, businesses, and non-profit organizations 'moving the world forward'.

greenblue.org
GreenBlue was founded by *Cradle to Cradle* authors William McDonough and Michael Braungart. It is now an autonomous nonprofit institute that helps professional communities create practical solutions, resources, and opportunities for implementing sustainability. They are a great resource if you are dealing with packaging or work for a large corporation that could afford to join their corporate partnerships.

idsa.org
IDSA is the site for The International Designers Society of America includes a section on ecodesign with resources and a blog listing.

indigodesignnetwork.org
INDIGO is an open network, connecting designers around the world with the goal of understanding the notion of indigenous design.

inhabitat.com
Inhabitat looks at the future of design and focuses on tracking the innovations in technology, practices and materials that are pushing architecture and home design towards a smarter and more sustainable future.

japanfs.org
Japan for Sustainability's site is available in both English and Japanese. It is not graphic design specific, but it is run by a group of people who are good at putting interested parties in touch with each other and giving general information about sustainability in Japan.

livingprinciples.org
The Living Principles aims to guide purposeful action, celebrating and popularizing the efforts of those who use design thinking to create positive cultural change.

lovelyasatree.com

Lovely as a Tree provides what a graphic designer needs to know in order to be more environmentally aware. It features a great interactive print finder feature that lets users choose by type of service and location.

metafore.org

MetaFore is linked to GreenBlue. The organization's Environmental Paper Assessment Tool (EPAT) provides consistent language and metrics for buyers and sellers of paper products to discuss the environmental ramifications of purchasing decisions. Note: MetaFore primarily works with large brand-name businesses.

o2.org

O2 Global Network is an international global network for sustainable issues. It is a great resource if you want to network with people working sustainably in your area or need information but live in an out-of-the way place. With new chapters popping up regularly, you can find people who are willing to talk, educate and share resources all over the world.

projecthdesign.org

Project H Design connects the power of design to the people who need it most, and the places where it can make a real and lasting difference.

re-nourish.com

Re-nourish is a US-based informational and networking site put together by Eric Benson. The site includes lists of green paper and printers; info on printing, paper, and packaging; and a case studies section. Re-nourish has its own blog, reprints articles, and offers lots of links to topics of interest.

sustainability.aiga.org

AIGA (The Professional Association for Design) provides information through case studies, interviews, resources, and discourse, to graphic designers who want to incorporate sustainable thinking into their professional lives.

sustainablecommunication.org

Institute for Sustainable Communication (ISC) helps advocate for and connect professionals and companies in the communications sector with tools that promote economic, social, and environmentally sound business practices. The Responsible Enterprise Print (REP) program, developed by the ISC, identifies opportunities for organizations to reduce costs, reduce environmental impacts, improve organizational effectiveness, and enhance stakeholder relationships.

sustainabledesignnet.org.uk

Sustainable Design Network is a UK-based research network that is part of the Sustainable Design Research Group at Loughborough Design School. SDN organizes one-day seminars related to sustainable issues.

sustainablepackaging.org

Sustainable Packaging Coalition, is an industry working group spinoff of GreenBlue.

themightyodo.com

Organic Design Operatives (ODO) is a diverse collective of creative people who are brought together by the common mission of connecting people with nature by design. The site offers an ecodesign tool kit, print spec worksheet, a networking feature, and there is a section on case studies.

treehugger.com

TreeHugger is a popular US-based sustainability website. The site includes articles on various environmental and social issues, products and programs as well as hosting annual Best of Green awards for initiatives and products in various sectors and categories.

vsointernational.org

VSO (Voluntary Services Organization) is a UK-based independent international development organization that works with volunteers to fight poverty in developing countries. The organization pairs volunteers with partners and NGOs that require specific skills.

Index

Picture credits

The author and publishers would like to thank the following for allowing us to use their materials.

7 concept and design: Kuhlmann Leavitt, Inc. Photo: Terry Heffernan. Client: NewPage Corporation;

9 Claudio Zaccherini/shutterstock.com;

14 Luis Stortini Sabor/shutterstock.com;

15 Concept and design: Kuhlmann Leavitt, Inc. Photo: Terry Heffernan. Client: NewPage Corporation;

16 courtesy of Ivy Chuang/Knoend;

17 courtesy of Kuhlmann Leavitt, Inc.;

18 © Idrissou Njoya/Ken'Art;

19 courtesy of MIO;

20 courtesy of Noah Scalin/Another Limited Rebellion © North Star Fund;

21 courtesy of Noah Scalin/ Another Limited Rebellion © Richmond Vegetarian Festival;

23 Worldpics/shutterstock.com; Grandpa/shutterstock.com;

24/25 courtesy of Toyota/Lexus;

26/27 courtesy of Noun Project/Creative Commons;

28 © Dan Whipps for The Nature Conservancy; courtesy of Bambeco;

29 Illustration by Chris Haughton, photo by Leonora Oppenheim;

32 courtesy of Siamak G. Shahneshin;

33 SHAGAL | iodaa; courtesy of Lui L. Galati;

34 courtesy of Siamak G. Shahneshin;

35 courtesy of Siamak G. Shahneshin;

36 courtesy of CURB Media Ltd;

39 courtesy of Frush; EU Ecolabel; E green logo; FSC;

41 courtesy of Shihwen Wang;

42 Is the Mediterranean Sea a Life's Sanctuary? Client: Good 50x70 designed by Sonia Diaz and Gabriel Martinez/Un Mundo Feliz, 2010;

43 Fully Grown, client Mediodia Chica Collective, designed by Sonia Diaz and Gabriel Martinez/ Un Mundo Feliz, 2010;

44 courtesy of GoodGuide;

56 courtesy of CURB Media Ltd;

57 Michael Eaton/ © 2010 Hyland's Inc.

58–61 courtesy of MIO;

62–65 courtesy of Bambeco;

66 © Idrissou Njoya/Ken'Art;

68 courtesy of Beyond Skin;

69 © People Tree, courtesy of PRshots.com;

70 courtesy of John Arndt Studio Gorm;

72 Iron Eyes Cody: 'People Start Pollution, People Can Stop It', campaign, 1971 Keep America Beautiful, Inc. (kab.org). Used with permission;

73 courtesy of Keep Britain Tidy;

74 Aflo Co. Ltd./Alamy;

75 courtesy of Brian Hurst;

76 © Aaris Sherin; © Jeffrey Barbee;

77–78 © Jeffrey Barbee;

79 courtesy of © Idrissou Njoya/Ken'Art;

80 © Dan Whipps for The Nature Conservancy; © Jay Zuckeron for The Nature Conservancy;

81 © Jay Zuckeron for The Nature Conservancy;

82–83 Sam Ogden/ Science Photo Library;

84–87 Singgih S. Kartonon/Magno;

90 environmantic/iStockphoto, Rich Carey/shutterstock.com;

91 © Ina Dimitrova;

94 © Disruptive Innovation Ltd 2012;

96 Roy Tam FRSA, Roy Tam Design, photo by Roy Tam;

98–103 courtesy of © Metalli Lindberg;

104 courtesy of Chris Haughton;

106 Photo by Noah Scalin © Christopher Humes/ Noah Scalin;

108–109 courtesy of Guido Styger | 2009;

111 courtesy of Memefest;

112–113 courtesy of Guido Styger | 2009; Jenna Layne Voigt/shutterstock;

114 courtesy of Emily Pilloton/Project H;

116–119 courtesy of Chris Haughton; courtesy of FLO, courtesy of WFTO;

120–121 courtesy of Forever Green Architects (project architect Dan Usiskin);

122–123 courtesy of Yoav Kotik;

126 Illustration by Chris Haughton;

127 courtesy of Nick Hancock Design Studio;

128–131 courtesy of Leonora Oppenheim;

134 courtesy of Chris Haughton;

126 Illustration by Chris Haughton;

127 courtesy of Nick Hancock Design Studio;

128–131 courtesy of Leonora Oppenheim;

134 courtesy of Chris Haughton;

136 © Aaris Sherin;

137 Fotographia INC./iStockphoto;

138–140 courtesy of frog design;

142-143 courtesy of Sidhika Sooklal (University of Pretoria – 2008);

144 courtesy of Zoe Murphy;

145 courtesy of Lou Rota;

146–49 © Aaris Sherin;

151 dotshock/shutterstock.com; spirit of America/shutterstock.com;

153 © Aaris Sherin; meunierd/shutterstock.com;

155 © Aaris Sherin;

156 courtesy of Sali Sasaki;

156 © UNESCO;

157 Design by Katsumi Asabi, photo by Kazumi Kurigami;

158 © UNESCO, concept and design by Sebastian Bettencourt; cover design by Saki Mafundikwa, courtesy Mark Batty Publisher;

162 concept and design: Kuhlmann Leavitt, Inc. Photo: Charles Shotwell. Client: NewPage Corporation;

169 courtesy of Scandanavian Business Seating;

171 Chamo/NODE;

179 courtesy of Marks and Spencer Plc.

Acknowledgements

This book is dedicated to my mother, Monika Sherin. My mother was a proponent of sustainable living before the term was ever connected with the environmental movement. During the first two decades of my life, my mother's insistence on saving and reusing everything from yogurt containers to tin foil was a source of ongoing annoyance. In the end, those values were contagious. Today, my own shelves are packed full of containers waiting a second, third, and fourth life in home projects and food storage. I thank my mother and many others who are drawn to make do with less and lead by example.

Thanks to Sali Sasaki and Fumi Masuda for introducing me to several of the designers whose work is featured in this text and to Liz Deluna, Betty Alfenito, and Alexander Gelfand for providing early feedback on the manuscript. This book was made more readable with help from Kathy McGee and I thank her for the time she spent working with me on the initial writing. Many thanks to Howard for all his support along the way and for always being willing to provide constructive criticism.

This book has been a collective effort and would not have been possible without the excellent team at Bloomsbury Publishing. Thanks to Caroline Walmsley and Georgia Kennedy for initially having faith in the project. I am deeply grateful to my editor, Kate Duffy, who spent countless hours working with me on the text, image selection and design edits. Finally, I want to thank the many designers, whose inspiring work has filled the pages of this book and made the text infinitely more interesting and relevant. Their work, ideas, and optimism provide evidence that lasting sustainable change is not only possible but is already in progress.